TRIGGERED TO *Heal*

An Invitation to Feel Fully and Heal Deeply

AMANDA D. LIGON, LMSW

NOTE TO THE READER

This book contains descriptions of childhood sexual abuse, sex trafficking, domestic violence, and other forms of trauma. Please care for yourself as you read. If you find yourself overwhelmed, it is okay to pause, step away, or seek support.

This book is my story woven from my lived experiences, personal reflections, and the healing practices that have supported my journey. As a Licensed Social Worker, I bring both professional training and lived experience to these pages. However, I share these truths not as prescriptions, but as invitations. What brought me strength and restoration may resonate with you, or it may not. Each healing journey is unique.

As you read, I invite you to take what serves you and gently release what does not. You are free to move at your own pace, pause when needed, and return when ready. This is your journey, and you are worthy of healing, restoration, and peace.

Please know that this book is not a substitute for professional therapy, medical care, or crisis intervention. While I am a licensed social worker, this book is a memoir and personal reflection, not a therapeutic relationship. If you are navigating trauma, abuse, or overwhelming emotions, I encourage you to seek guidance from licensed therapists, counselors, or trusted support systems. Your safety and well-being matter. If you are in crisis, please reach out for immediate help:

- National Domestic Violence Hotline: 1-800-799-7233 (SAFE) | Text "START" to 88788 | thehotline.org
- National Sexual Assault Hotline: 1-800-656-4673 (HOPE) | rainn.org
- 988 Suicide & Crisis Lifeline: Call or text 988 | 988lifeline.org

With love and solidarity,
Amanda

TABLE OF CONTENTS

PART THREE AWAKENING MY VOICE

Breaking silence, reclaiming agency, and choosing peace for the first time.

PART FOUR TRANSFORMATION

Ending cycles, healing deeply, and finding wisdom in the very pain that once defined.

DEDICATION

I dedicate this book to every adult who silently survived childhood sexual abuse. I honor your resilience, your hidden pain, and the sacred strength it took to keep going when giving up felt easier.

To my double M&M's and Bonus M, you are the reason I broke the secret cycle of silence. You are my why, my breath, my hope, and my sunlight.

My dear friend of over twenty years, Mr. Tennant, thank you for being a friend, always encouraging me to do my best, and always believing in me.

And to you, the reader, may these pages meet you with compassion and courage for your own journey.

FOREWORD

Amanda's courage is a gift for all of us. She has done a masterful job of telling her story of terror and then showing us how to survive those tragedies. Not only does she show us how to survive, but she goes on to show us how to succeed beyond what we thought was possible. This is a must-read for clients and practitioners!

—James H. Riley, LCSW, CCTP

INTRODUCTION

Have you ever been judged by your past or even by your present and felt that judgment linger like a shadow just behind you?

Sometimes that shadow doesn't look like sadness. Sometimes it explodes as anger, violence, anxiety, or depression. Sometimes it hides beneath drinking, smoking, overspending, multiple sex partners, overworking, or shutting down; all subconscious attempts to escape the shadow you didn't know was following you.

This book is my story. Raw, unfiltered, and real. It's about the moments that broke me, the shadows that almost buried me, and the truths that set me free. It's about the little girl who was abandoned, abused, exploited, and who grew into an adult convinced she deserved continued pain. For over 20 years, I allowed harm into my life because my unhealed trauma was longing to be wanted.

For years, I believed silence was my shield, that if I never spoke my pain, it might simply dissolve, or fade into the background like a forgotten dream. But pain never disappears. Pain never truly leaves the body. It waits. It lingers. It whispers. It surfaces in relationships, in boundaries, in the way we see ourselves. It trembles in our hands, hides in our breath, and lingers when we feel unseen, even when surrounded by people.

I don't share my story because it's easy. I share it because I believe healing is contagious.

If you've ever been told to "get over it," let me tell you something different: you don't need to get over it, you need to grow through it. And you don't have to grow through it alone. When one of us rises, we remind others that rising is possible.

Healing isn't linear. It isn't neat or pretty. It is messy, sacred, and deeply personal.

My journey taught me that we cannot fully heal until we acknowledge our feelings and allow ourselves to feel everything we've buried: the anger, the loneliness, the grief, the betrayal, and even the love we longed for but never received.

Before I could heal, I had to anchor myself in something greater than my pain. For me, that anchor was faith. I learned that God had always been with me—in the breath I drew when I thought I couldn't, in the stillness when I finally stopped running, in the quiet assurance that I was seen, known, and loved.

Faith didn't erase my trauma, but it gave me footing to face it. Scripture became my lifeline. Prayer became my refuge. And knowing I was never alone gave me the courage to continue.

Oftentimes, while writing this book, I had to stop, walk away, and sit with what I had lived through. Though I have learned to feel fully and heal deeply from what I survived, I could not include everything I experienced. What I've discovered through this invitation to heal is that being related to someone or in relationship with them does not mean they love you. It doesn't guarantee respect, kindness, or protection. I've learned that the most important relationship is the one you have with yourself. I taught myself to love, respect, show kindness to, and protect me.

Now, I am surrounded by people who love, respect, are kind, and look out for me. I am fully persuaded that the people who surround you are a reflection of how you feel about yourself.

This book is my story, the what and the why. Yet it is more than that; it is an invitation. An invitation to step into your own healing, to remember you are not alone, to feel fully, heal deeply, and reclaim the truth that your voice, your story, and your life matter.

If you're wondering how I healed, I've created a companion workbook called *Triggered to Heal Workbook: 16 Sacred Practices to Heal Deeply*. In it, I share the practices—breath, prayer, movement, therapy, creativity, and more—that carried me from survival to wholeness. This memoir invites you into my journey, and the workbook invites you into your own healing.

So, turn the page. Not only to read my journey, but to awaken your own.

PART ONE
SHADOWS

A trigger is more than an overreaction—
it is a body's alarm, signaling pain that
has not yet been healed.
—Amanda D. Ligon

THE INVITATION

*Every trigger is an invitation to a part of
you still waiting to be seen and heard.*

"**B**ut Peaches, you used to be a prostitute!" The words hit me like a punch to the chest as we rode in the car after a birthday celebration. My palms began to sweat. My heart raced. My lips trembled. My hands balled into fists. I had never been in a fight before, but in that moment, rage and disbelief surged through me with the weight of a thousand buried truths clawing their way out.

With every spark of fire in my voice, I demanded, "Where did you get that from? Who told you that?" This wasn't the first time I heard this person making this false statement. I remembered her telling the same lie to a young woman I mentored spiritually twenty years ago. My voice rose again, sharper now: "Where did you get that from? Who told you that? Because I was never a prostitute! I never did drugs! I didn't even have my first drink until 2019, when I was in my forties."

Then she fired back, as if trying to prove something: "But Peaches, weren't you having sex at eleven?"

Those words weren't just a question. They were a weapon, an accusation that cut straight into my deepest wound. Eleven wasn't a memory of consent. It was a memory of violation. It was the age I felt like every living being craved me, and not in a way that made me feel wanted or safe. My ears burned. My body tightened. My mind screamed. I wanted to jump on top of the car, scream out loud, and run down the street. I wanted to fight.

Instead, I chose truth. Because this person had triggered me before with their slanderous statements. I did not shrink. I did not swallow my words. And I did not let the moment slip away. This time, I refused to ignore the false story this person continues to share with others about who I was a child and what I had lived through. Without hesitation, I stood in the truth of what I had survived and allowed my voice to rise. I raised my voice loud enough for the little girl inside me to feel defended. "First of all, this is not a conversation to have in front of your spouse. But since you brought it up, I was never a prostitute! And I don't consider an eleven-year-old as capable of consenting to sex, because they can't! An eleven-year-old is either being molested, raped, or sex trafficked. I was a child being used, sold, and abused to supply my mother's needs: money, drugs, alcohol, rent, cigarettes, clothes, food."

Without second thought to the person's spouse, I shared my horrific experiences of not only surviving molestation, rape, and sex trafficking, but also the fact that my mother began having sex with me. In my haste, I spoke with authority, claiming that my last piece of safety had been stolen. At the age of eleven was when my mother came into my room. Not to ask me to do "another sexual favor" for an adult neighbor or friend. But to feed her distorted sexual desires.

Then I questioned my accuser, "And where were you? Were you there? Where were you when I was just a child? I swear I only remember seeing you a handful of times growing up. And what gives you the right to speak on and share with others what you did not witness? How could you pass that lie around for twenty years when you were not present? How can you share things about me without verifying its accuracy? And how can you talk about what happened to me when I was an innocent child?"

She nonchalantly replied, "Well, I'm sure my mommy or my aunt told me because that's what I heard, that you were a prostitute, strung out on drugs and alcohol." For a moment, everything stopped. Not the car. Not the world around me. But something deep inside me froze. I was triggered again. I wasn't fully conscious of it, but I heard myself reply, "My goodness, what a tragic commentary on the adults who not only speculated that about me when I was an innocent child, but actually voiced those opinions aloud, as if what I was suffering was juicy gossip, and never once reported their suspicions to Child Protective Services. How heartbreaking that grown people could talk about a child that way, and still do nothing to protect her." Then she said, "Well, weren't you having sex? They obviously picked up on you having sex; that's why they said you were a prostitute."

I sat in complete disbelief. This person, a mother, an educator, a trauma-informed life coach, was justifying why adults had labeled me a "prostitute," while simultaneously shaming me. As if I somehow deserved the accusation. As if I had earned that label as an innocent child.

Whether this person's intent was malicious, ignorant, or just careless, I was triggered. For those who may not fully understand what that means, being triggered is not simply about feeling upset or offended; it is a more complex experience. It is a sudden, intense emotional and physical reaction that pulls you back into a past trauma, as if it is happening all over again. In the moment, your body does not realize the danger has passed. According to the American Psychological Association (n.d.), a trigger is "a stimulus that elicits a reaction," one that can resurface the memories and emotional weight of earlier traumatic experiences. For survivors, the nervous system responds with overwhelming sensations such as fear, shame, rage, or sometimes complete numbness. That is because the brain perceives the present moment as a mirror of past harm (van der Kolk, 2014).

Triggers can come in many forms: a word, a smell, a facial expression, even a particular tone of voice. And suddenly, your entire system is hijacked. It goes far beyond emotion. It's as if your body and mind have time-traveled to the original moment of trauma, even though you may be physically safe now.

If you have ever found yourself shaking, dissociating, or shutting down for reasons you could not quite name, you are not imagining it. These reactions are not "just in your head." They are real and are part of your body's survival system, the autonomic nervous system, which activates the fight, flight, or freeze responses to protect you. Even when your mind knows you're safe, your body might not realize it right away. Neuroscientist Stephen Porges (2011), through his *Polyvagal* Theory, explains that the autonomic nervous system constantly scans the environment for cues of safety or danger. Depending on whether the body senses safety or threat, it shifts between states of social connection, mobilization (fight or flight), or immobilization (freeze).

What I experienced in that car was not an overreaction; it was biology. My nervous system was doing exactly what it was designed to do: protect me. That moment in the car wasn't just emotional; it was physical. My body responded as if I were in danger all over again. It felt as if time collapsed, and I was not a grown woman riding in that car. I became that little girl again. Confused. Exposed. Unprotected. That sudden, humiliating, and defamatory comment, "But Peaches, you used to be a prostitute," hit a deep nerve tied to my earliest trauma. It was not just the words. It was what they represented. A repeated accusation, shame, judgment, betrayal, defamation, all crashing in simultaneously.

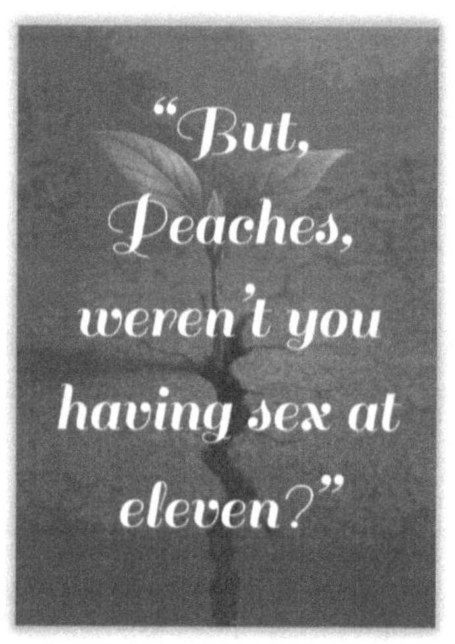

That triggering experience lingered for minutes, hours, days, and weeks. The deep sorrow and shame I experienced silenced me. Repeatedly, I heard the words, *"But Peaches, you used to be a prostitute! But Peaches, weren't you having sex at eleven? Oh, I thought you were strung out. Well, they must have thought you were having sex. Well, it gives your testimony that much more power."* Whew, as if I ever needed that person's help telling my story. As if their slanderous accusations somehow added value to my truth.

Instead of attempting to silence my trigger, by impulsive habits of charging up my credit cards through shopping, fine dining, gift giving, booking a trip, or calling an ex-boyfriend with the subconscious attempt to release

Oxytocin to feel wanted. I leaned into what had triggered me to understand why I felt such sorrow and shame. It was uncomfortable. For weeks, nearly every day, I screamed and cried as I reflected on what I lived through. Until one morning, still in emotional pain, I asked myself why I was feeling shame. After pondering this question for several hours, I began questioning the deep bouts of sorrow. Suddenly, empowering questions came to mind. What am I supposed to learn from this? Why has this re-surfaced now? I realized this experience was not an accident or a coincidence. It had come to serve me. It was an invitation to confront, feel, reflect, release, and ulti-mately heal.

I was able to embrace what I endured in my youth was not my fault! There was no longer a need to walk in shame and condemnation as if I had done something wrong. For the first time in my life, the negative, evil, malicious words that had shaped how I saw myself, and what I assumed others thought about me lost their power! Through this trigger, I was given the gift to see myself for who I truly am. This experience did not make me shutdown or hide in shame. Instead, I saw myself, not as a victim, but as a Survivor!

With the intention of healing, I began releasing my truth on paper. It was not easy. Often, I had to walk away, because I couldn't see the paper through my tears. But I kept releasing my sorrow and shame. Through writing. Crying. Running in the park. Playing tennis. Tapping into creativity. Talking with trusted friends. Connecting with a therapist (thank you, Charissa). Drinking lots of water. Taking long hot baths and a few cold showers. Going to church. Offering kindness and service for others. Most of all, I learned to be gentle with myself. To extend compassion to the little girl in me who survived!

Being triggered was not about shame. It was not a sign that I was to blame for the severe sexual child abuse I endured. It was not a declaration that I am broken, or "F'ed up" because of my childhood, as my ex-husband often told me. And it was certainly not a reason to silence my truth. Being triggered was an invitation to respond to my body's feelings.

Whatever narrative someone else has about what you experienced or survived does not make it

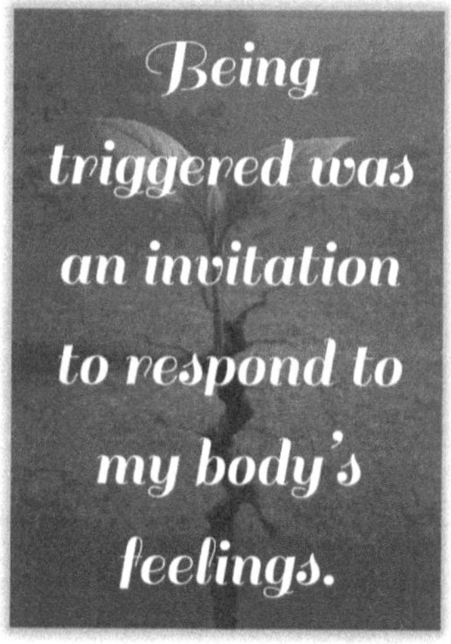

accurate. No one knows your story better than you, because you lived it. And you survived it. Every inappropriate touch. Every label. Every bruise. Every scar. Every tear. Every moment of terror. You were there. The pain did not just vanish. Your body carries the evidence. It settled into your skin, your muscles, and your breath. It occupied space in your psyche, your identity, and your self-worth. It became part of your spirit, your soul, your fingerprints, and your footprints.

Being triggered is not a weakness. It is a signal, a divine alert that something within you is still asking to be seen. When I stopped silencing myself and chose curiosity over judgment, I discovered something I never expected: a doorway into my own healing. What began as sorrow and rage transformed into words on a page, and eventually into this book.

Triggered to Heal is more than a title. It is my lived truth, an invitation to feel fully, to heal deeply, and to reclaim the voice I was once forced to silence.

And so, I accepted the invitation.

—2—

TO FEEL FULLY

*What you refuse to feel will quietly rule
your life until you let it rise.*

With the invitation to feel fully and heal deeply, I drew myself a hot bubble bath, lit a few candles, dropped in one of my homemade bath tea bags, and asked myself with curiosity: What feelings of pain have I recently hushed or left unprocessed?

Within minutes, a memory surfaced. A few years ago, I was raped by someone I knew. At the time, I was working with survivors of sexual assault every day, yet I didn't report what happened to me to the authorities. I didn't even tell my closest friend. Instead, I convinced myself it was somehow my fault. After all, I went to his home late one evening. I told myself, "What did you expect? You knew he wanted to have sex." He had made comments about wanting to have sex with me a few times in the past.

I gave up the tug of war over my pants and surren-dered my will. When he was finished, he apologized and said, "What did you ex-pect coming over here looking and smelling so damn good?" He got up, got a wash rag, and pro-ceeded to wipe me off. I lay quiet and numb. He asked

if I was okay, I whispered "yes" and put my pants back on. He walked me to my car and said, "See I am a gen-tleman, you should give me a chance so we can date." With a half-smile, I said thanks and got in my car. That was the longest 25-minute drive home in silence.

The next morning while at work, I hushed my own pain and kept my focus on the safety of the clients we served. I never reported the incident because of the shame I had going to his home so late in the evening. I had convinced myself no one would believe me. And if I'm being honest with myself, the act of surrendering; of being forced into unwanted sexual acts, was painfully fa-miliar.

When I was nineteen, I remember sitting with a tutor who was helping me prepare for the Ohio Graduation State Test. She asked about my life, and I told her I had a two-year-old son and my own apartment. Somewhere in that conversation, I shared that my mom used to sell me for drugs when I was a little girl.

For a moment, the tutor's face froze. "Oh, my goodness," she said. "Did you ever report that? Did CPS get involved? Did you have counseling afterward?"

My answers were all the same: No. No. And no. I also told her it wasn't a big deal. I shrugged it off. It was just life. But she looked me in the eye, touched my hand gently, and said words I will never forget: "That was and is a big deal. And that is not a normal life." Her words cut through years of silence. She encouraged me to seek counseling, even if I wasn't ready to report my mother.

Week after week, she asked if I had made an appointment. Finally, I called to schedule an appointment. I sat in front of a therapist at a Children's Hospital Mental Health Center, and I shut down. The therapist asked about my past, and I didn't understand why revisiting my history mattered. To me, the pain had been locked away for so long it felt irrelevant, just a part of life I had survived.

To feel fully,

I began to see how my unprocessed experiences kept me walking into familiar pain. Not because I deserved it, and not because being raped a few years ago was ever justified, but because I hadn't processed, released, or healed what began in my youth. My body remembered. My nervous system carried the echoes. And without realizing it, I became an energetic match for the same emotions I first felt as a child: secrecy, fear, shame, feeling unprotected, and believing it was somehow normal.

Feeling fully showed me something I had spent years running from: the past does not vanish simply because we silence it. What we do not process waits for us, often resurfacing in moments we least expect. My body carried echoes I never asked for, and those echoes drew me back into familiar patterns of secrecy, fear, and shame.

But feeling fully also gave me the courage to name what was happening inside me, to stop pretending, to stop minimizing, and to finally allow the truth to rise. I realized that every unspoken moment of pain was an invitation, not to blame myself, but to acknowledge the pain I was feeling. And this is what it meant to feel fully: not to drown in my past, but to face it with honesty and compassion. As trauma researcher Peter Levine (1997) explains, unresolved trauma lingers in the body until it is acknowledged and released.

Feeling fully was my first step in that release. Responding to the sensations in my body without shame and letting them guide me back to the places where the lies were planted was where healing deeply truly began.

$$-3-$$

PLANTED SEEDS

The stories we bury in silence don't
disappear; they grow roots.

What happened in that car didn't begin there. The echoes I felt while learning to feel fully were not new, they were rooted deep in my beginnings. To understand why her words unraveled me so deeply, I had to return to the first lie I was told about who I was. To the first touch. To the first wound. Before I could heal, I had to remember.

From birth to the age of three, my memory is a void. There is nothing to trace or hold onto. But around three and a half, awareness came, and with it, pain. An uncle touched me in secret. His hands were a silent violation that stretched from my earliest memories into my teenage years.

At four, my mother reappeared. There was no warmth. No familiar scent. No feeling of homecoming or maternal love. Just a woman whose words would plant themselves deep in my subconscious, shaping what I believed about myself.

She said, "The moment the doctor placed you in my arms, I did not want you. I thought you were an ugly baby. You had big eyes, a big ol' head, a small body, and you were covered in fine, fuzzy hair. You looked just like Tweety Bird, the small yellow cartoon bird with the oversized head from Warner Bros. So, I named you 'Tweety,' but one of my siblings said, 'No, do not name her Tweety. Name her Peaches. She looks like a peach with all that fuzz on her.' And so, because you were covered in fuzz, I agreed and nicknamed you Peaches." That was the moment a seed was planted: the belief that I was an ugly baby who was not wanted.

That is what my four-year-old ears heard and tried to process, not just in that moment, but many years after. I did not realize it then, but those words planted a perennial seed in me, one that would take a lifetime to comprehend.

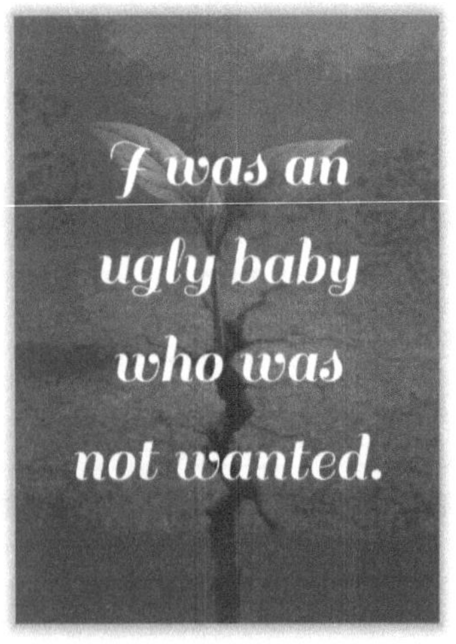

I felt ugly and unwanted. Whenever I saw my reflection, I could not help but focus on my big eyes, forehead, and skinny body. I avoided mirrors because they intensified the feeling of unworthiness, and I did not want to be reminded. Still, my mother taught me things even in the shadows of rejection.

In a short time, my mother taught me how to read, braid my hair, wash my back, scrub my knees and elbows, brush my teeth with baking soda, hold a baby, wash dishes, boil chicken, and even do a headstand. By six, her lessons turned cruel. She started cursing at me and calling me names. Hitting me. Leaving me alone for hours. Dropping me off at her friends' or family's house.

One weekend, when an adult male cousin brought me home, he looked at my mother, pointed at my neck, and said, "Look at your fast-ass little girl." I stood there confused, because this same cousin had been molesting me. I had a hickey on my neck, a love bite from one of his siblings, another abuser. My mother did not ask what happened. She did not demand answers. She just beat me so badly I could not move my right hand. The next morning, as I stood at the kitchen sink, she beat me again and then threw me out of the house for not washing the dishes fast enough. "Wait on the front porch for Ms. B.J. to pick you up," she said. "Since you can't wash dishes and want to be a fast-ass little girl." I did not know my wrist was broken. She did not care.

For about two weeks, I stayed with my mom's close friend, Ms. B.J., before she took me back home. During that time, she noticed my wrist wasn't getting better, so she picked up my mom and drove us both to the local Children's Hospital. Not one adult asked me how my wrist had been broken: not the ER doctor, not my teacher, not even Ms. B.J. No one asked, and I didn't tell.

By nine, something inside me came to understand that this was my childhood, and it was not going to change. One summer, as I was transitioning from fourth to fifth grade, my mother was beating me, just as she always did when coming down from one of her drug and alcohol binges. Desperate, I grabbed one end of the extension cord and cried out, "Please kill me! I cannot take it anymore." For a moment, everything was still. The earth itself seemed to pause. Then, suddenly, my mother reared her arm back, ripped the extension cord from my small hands, and snarled, "Bitch, you want to die?" Even now, as I type this, I can feel its force, the sting of the cord landing on my head, the back of my neck, and my shoulders.

The impact reverberated through my body. My mother struck me harder, with more rage, repeatedly, each blow punctuated by the exact words, "Bitch, you want to die?" My childhood consisted of beatings with extension cords, iron cords, thick leather belts, trick tracks, wire hangers, thick switches, shoes, open-handed slaps, punches, and kicks. The names became their own weapons, Bitch! You ugly bitch! Slut! Whore! Fast-ass little girl! Stupid! Dumbass! Judging by her heavy-handed strikes, coupled with her words, it felt like she was trying to rid the ugly out of me.

By ten, I had been sexually violated by countless adults, including a woman who was a grandmother. I knew things no child should know. I knew that pubic hair could be black or white. I saw it. Even now, I cannot prove this, but no one can convince me otherwise. I know what I saw.

I also knew that people wore invisible masks. Adults smiled and acted trustworthy. But I could feel they were pretending because others were watching. Beneath their masks, I sensed something dark, an unspoken hunger. I did not have the language then, but I knew it was dangerous. I could not understand how adults could shift and change, wearing different faces. So instead of speaking up, I buried what I knew. I buried my intuition and moved through my childhood in fear.

The seed of rejection my mother planted took root. It choked out any belief that I could be loved or protected. When I was left alone with a predator, I told myself it was because I was ugly. When I was first molested, I believed it was my fault because of how I looked.

I can recall when my mother walked out the front door of Mr. Bee's home after the two whispered back and forth. Before he locked the front door, I instinctively perceived he was not a safe person. At eight, my mother did not have to tell me not to put up a fight or resist Mr. Bee. Without my mother's coaching, I knew what to do to make her happy. When my mother returned to pick me up from Mr. Bee's, she would not even look at me. I did not know if she was mad at me or Mr. Bee. The two of them would always go into the kitchen and whisper. My mother would then say to me, "Come on." Walking back across the field, I was always unsure if my mom was happy or upset. The walk wasn't far, but the silence made it feel endless. I lost count of how many times we walked that same path home from Mr. Bee's.

During my adolescent years, she continued to exploit me. She allowed adults to have their way with me, including the man listed on my birth certificate. Being preyed upon felt normal. It felt like the reason I existed.

Eventually, my mother began having sex with me, too.

One night, when I was eleven, she came into my room, not to send me to someone else, but for herself. "Come downstairs," she said. I did. "Lean back on the couch." I did. She said she had wanted to do this "for me" for a long time. That couch. Goldishtan, flower-print, two-piece couch set, donated to us by a charity agency. The unbreakable plastic cover was still on it.

Even today, I can still smell the alcohol on her breath. The stale ashes in the ashtray on the floor. I was wearing a white camisole and panties. She told me not to tell anyone, or let the woman across the field know, or allow her to do this to me.

And yet, as she warned me about the woman across the field, she was taking my panties down. She kept saying she had been wanting to do this for me. She lit a cigarette. Took a swig from her 40 oz. It seemed both our hearts were pounding, but for different reasons. Her heart was pounding with excitement, mine with fear. And although adults having their way with me sexually felt normal, there was just something about my mother's sexual touch that felt abnormal.

Yet, I leaned back on the couch, not because I was comfortable, but because I did not know what else to do. I did not know how to say no or even if saying no was an option. My body froze between confusion and fear, as her hands, her fingers, and her lips touched me in ways I never imagined my mother could. My mind went quiet, like I had slipped beneath the surface of water. I could feel her pulling my panties from around my feet. I saw the cigarette smoke. I smelled her breath. I heard her whispering. I did not understand the words. She whispered things I did not understand. And as I lay there confused and afraid, what hurt the most was that deep down, I had longed for her touch. For her attention. For her love. But not like this. Never like this.

When my mother stopped and I saw her face again, she asked if I wanted to lay with her on the couch. I slowly shook my head "no." My mother was sitting on the floor in between my legs, when she then scooted back a little, closed my legs, and said I can go back to my room. I stood up feeling like I had peed on myself as I looked for my panties. My mother handed me my panties and said, "Don't forget not to tell anyone." I nodded my head "yes" in agreement and walked away in the dark, yet not stumbling because of the moonlight coming through the curtains. As I walked up the steps, I counted

13 steps, holding my panties in my right hand, and feeling what I understood at the time: my vagina and my inner thighs sweating. There were no thoughts, only numbness for this was my normal.

During my adolescent life, I was so vibrationally low that I wanted to die. Living with my mother was a cycle of fear, pain, and shame. It was suffocating. It was unbearable. It was utterly, inescapably sad. By fifteen, my mother was still physically, sexually, and verbally abusing, and exploiting me. I had been raped several times at gunpoint, held at knifepoint, and beaten. Sexual violence was my normal. Yet even in what was my norm, there was a small truth whispering that life wasn't meant to be this way. I didn't know how to act on those whispers, I just felt sparks of hope. A kind of hope that would suggest that somewhere beyond my mother, there was a better way to live.

Sometimes I wonder why I kept silent. Why I went along with my mother as she waited in another room while I performed sexual favors to feed her drug addiction. Why couldn't I refuse her sexual advances? Why couldn't I fight off predators? Why couldn't I say no? When I was nearly sixteen, why didn't I stay gone when I hitchhiked three states away? I wonder where my protector was, the fighter I desperately needed. So many questions. So many "*whys*" I could not answer. And beneath all of them, tangled in the silence, wrapped in fear, was love for my mother. After all, she was my mother.

During the brief time she spent teaching me life

skills, she often shared the pain of her childhood. I was too young to fully understand, let alone grasp, the depth of what she had been through. But I felt her sadness. I felt her pain. And despite my age, that sadness made me want to be close to her and be there for her.

From infancy, my craving to be wanted and held by my mother created an energy that released an aroma that begged for connection. I was wired to associate any touch with attachment. Even when touch was abusive, my body responded. The oxytocin released during abuse created a confusing bond. Research shows that oxytocin, often called the "bonding hormone," plays a role in attachment even when the relationship is harmful (Feldman, 2012). It wasn't love. But it felt like a connection.

Subconsciously, I associated any touch with being wanted. Even though I believed I was being molested and raped because I was ugly, somewhere beneath the inappropriate touches, I felt a distorted sense of connection. The feeling of being connected taught me how to use my words, which kept me alive. I learned how to talk predators down. I reasoned with men who threatened me with guns and knives for fear of exposure.

Creatively, I am alive to tell my story because I

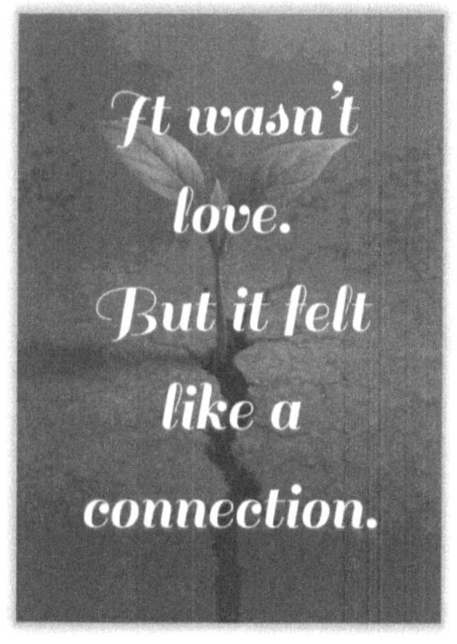

tapped into something within me that wanted to live. Many may ask, "Well, why didn't you tap into that same something and tell someone you were being raped?" I never said anything because I did not fully understand it was wrong. It was my norm, and a part of me felt I deserved it. I always felt ashamed because I was born ugly and my mother did not want me. And I had genuine fear that harm would come if I said anything. My mother was physically, verbally, and sexually abusing and exploiting me. Normalcy and fear co-existed and shaped my outlook on molestation and rape.

Without realizing it, I grew up learning how to operate from the space of fear and abuse. My body became conditioned to associate being abused with being wanted. By the time I became an adult, the violence and violations I endured had shaped my very being, making me a vibrational match for others who would continue my fear, suffering, and silence.

PART TWO

THE BREAKING

Fear disguised as love teaches silence
until truth finds its voice.
—Amanda D. Ligon

4

THE BETRAYAL OF BIOLOGY

Sometimes the body bonds to what broke it,
until love rewrites the pattern.

That conditioning didn't stay in childhood, it followed me into adulthood. Without awareness, I found myself drawn to a relationship that mirrored the pain I already knew. I entered a relationship with a man ten years my senior. After knowing him for only nine days, I bought him a gift to celebrate him being a father. He belittled my gesture and said, "This is the dumbest gift I've ever received." He looked at the roses I had picked out carefully and said, "Everyone knows not to buy roses, they die within a few days."

While he had not physically abused me at that point, he was already emotionally abusive. Looking back now, he often made comments that were glaring red flags. He mocked my "junky car," referred to my apartment as "the hood," and made colorist remarks like, "I never thought

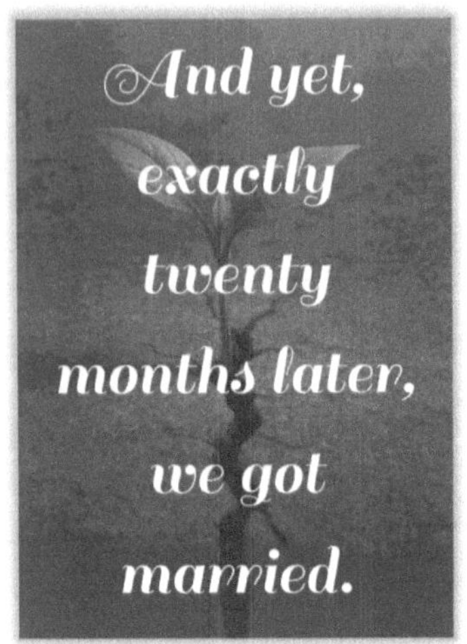

I'd talk to a light-skinned, tall woman." He reminded me more than once that I was not his type, that he was not attracted to me, because his preference was "short and dark-skinned, or at least brown-skinned."

And yet, exactly twenty months later, we got married.

On our wedding night, oxytocin and dopamine surged through my body like a celebration. Every part of me, every nerve ending, every pulse, was alive with joy and intimacy. My body would have testified: I was excited, happy, and in love with my husband. But my intuition told another story.

It whispered that my husband was not nearly as thrilled to be with his wife. I remember trying to kiss him and sensing the hesitation in his lips. The way he kissed me back, if he kissed me back, felt forced. But I did not let that stop me. I kept kissing him. I touched him, climbed on top of him, and tried to give him all the love my body held. I remember him saying, "Damn, you're dripping all over me, man… where's a towel?" Embarrassed, I apologized and pressed my legs together in between his. That is when it happened; his body stiffened, not in arousal, but in rejection. His silence said what his words never did: Get off me. I am not feeling you and still I kept making love to my husband.

I sensed he did not want to be married from that very night. And from that moment forward, I could feel it in his energy that I was unwanted. Over twenty years, my husband called me other women's names while having sex with me. He forced sex on me. He hit me. He smacked me. He squeezed my jaw until the inside of my mouth bled. He beat me with a belt. He locked me out of the house.

He called me derogatory names and tore down everything I was. He told me I was fat. I was ugly. I was too light-skinned. He was not attracted to me. He said my pussy was too wet. That it should be dry by now, "since you've been getting dick since you were three." He said I was dumb. Weak. I did not know how to grocery shop. I did not know how to pick fresh fruit. Nobody really liked me. I did not have any real friends. That I would not have anything if it were not for him. He would mock me, saying I did not know what a father was because I never had one.

He refused to take me or even go with me to doctor's appointments when I needed support. On three different occasions, after I had been rushed to the hospital by ambulance, he refused to pick me up. Each time, he would say, "Get home the same way you got there." Once, my back gave out and I could not walk. I was in so much pain, I asked him to take me to the emergency room. He said he was not taking off work. I told him I needed to call 911. He threatened me: "If you call 911 and embarrass me, I'll hurt you." By God's grace, hours later, I managed to crawl into my vehicle, drive to the end of my street, and call 911. The ambulance came and took me to the emergency room.

Even while I was pregnant, he would hit me, force sex on me, and threaten to kill me. When I was carrying our oldest child, he held a hot iron near my face and threatened to burn me like my mother. Throughout our marriage, he forced sex on me more times than I can count. He would threaten, "I'm going to put it in your ass if you don't open your legs." He forced his penis in my mouth, repeatedly. After I gave birth to our second child, he tried to rape me to get me pregnant again. He said the baby was not his, "He's too light-skinned." He kept asking, "Why do people keep saying the baby looks like you and not me? I want a DNA test." I agreed. I found a company that would do the DNA test for $400 and scheduled the appointment myself. A couple of days before the test, he said, "Just give me the $400 and I will not bring it up again. I know the baby's mine." But I was not going to give him a reason to sexually assault me, beat up on, or be told our son was not his, because of his doubts. So, I kept the appointment. I gave the company *the* $400. And the test proved what I already knew: He was the father, 99.999999% without question.

Instead of seeing my oldest son as an opportunity to be a great bonus father, my ex-husband was verbally, emotionally, and physically abusive toward him. Before

I met my husband, I had a beautiful two-year-old son who was gentle, well-behaved, joyful, and obedient. When he was a toddler, I could tell him, "It's nap time," "Bedtime," "Time to stop playing," or even "No," and he would not fall out or cry. He would go with the flow. He trusted my voice. He followed my lead. He was peace in motion. It saddens me that a man I loved so deeply could be so cruel to my son-light. My son was innocent. Bright. A joy to be around. It was just me and him in our little world for two years. His presence lit up every room he entered. He was the kind of baby and toddler who flowed easily with everyone and everything around him.

So, I often wonder: Why would my husband sneak behind my back and tell this amazing little boy that he was bad? That his mother was ashamed of him? That his father didn't love him, that's why he never came to see him? How do I know he said those things?

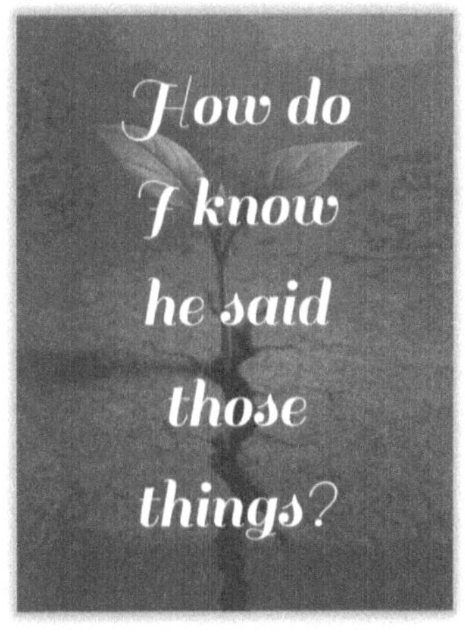

When my son was in the tenth grade, he wrote me a ten-page letter, crying out for help. In it, he begged for us to go back to our apartment in Gahanna, so that "the monster" could not abuse us anymore. He wrote, "Mommy, this is not right. This is not how we are supposed to live. We are supposed to be happy." At this time, our oldest child, his biological daughter, was long gone, grown, and living on her own. So, I found the courage to leave. For real this time. My two children and I moved out. But it did not end there. My husband came to my home daily, coercing me sexually. Eventually, I got pregnant, and because of this, my two children and I moved back in with him.

If you're reading this, you may wonder. Why did I move my children and I out to move back in? Why did I return and stay for nearly ten more years? Why did I remain with a man who was so cruel, not just to me, but especially to my innocent child and our unborn children?

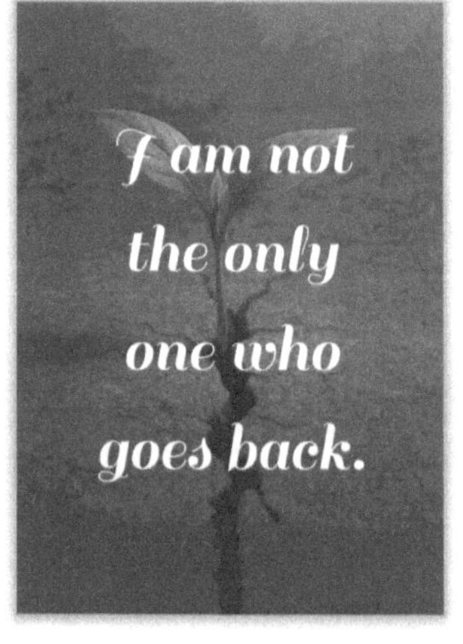

Research shows that on average, it takes a victim seven attempts to leave an abusive relationship for good. Seven cycles of trying, hoping, fearing, and returning before they finally break free (Domestic Violence Center of Chester County, n.d.). And tragically, the violence often escalates with every return. Since I was a little girl, I had vivid dreams of being thirty years old, married, with two children, a boy and a girl. And despite all the negative things he said about me, I held on to that dream. And in some painful way, I was happy that the picture I had always imagined had finally come to life. My dream had come true. At least, that is what I kept telling myself.

Yet that is not entirely true for me. I stayed because fear and pain were more familiar to me than peace. After suffering so much trauma in my youth, I could not perceive another way of existing. My internal compass was distorted. I was operating from a place where fear felt familiar and pain felt normal. I had unknowingly come to associate those emotions with connection. To be hurt meant to be noticed. To feel pain meant I wasn't alone.

It was a betrayal of biology, a chemical comfort that reinforced my trauma. Let me explain. When I speak of a betrayal of biology, I am naming the painful irony that the very chemicals designed to help us feel safe, loved, and bonded, like oxytocin, are released during moments of trauma. Even in an unsafe or abusive environment, oxytocin is still autonomically released through physical touch or emotional proximity (Olff et al., 2013). And because oxytocin is so closely tied to bonding and attachment, the nervous system can begin to associate pain with intimacy and love with harm. This is the betrayal.

Your body does exactly what it was designed to do. It releases oxytocin to help you feel soothed, connected, and less alone. But when that release happens in the context of a violation, it creates a chemical comfort that blurs the line between danger and closeness. It eases the ache of isolation, but at the cost of reinforcing trauma patterns. Over time, your nervous system learns: this is what closeness feels like. And later in life, your body may crave that same pattern, not because you want to be hurt, but because it's the only form of connection your body has known (Martins et al., 2022).

This is why it took me years to break free from the abuse of my ex-husband. To end the cycle of domestic violence. To silence the words he used to justify his harm. To stop believing I deserved it. To finally untangle love from pain. It also meant letting go of the guilt I carried for my mother, no longer romanticizing her suffering, or excusing her behaviors. I had to unlearn what my body had been trained to expect: that connection required me to endure harm.

I was not drawn to abuse because I wanted it, as my ex-husband always accused me of, but because my body had never experienced affection without fear. I had been pre-wired to seek closeness, even if that closeness came through violation. From my earliest years, oxytocin, the chemical comforter, taught me to connect for survival, not to bond for love. Through repeated exposure, my nervous system learned that pain is where connection lives.

It did not happen overnight. It took nearly eighty-seven months of one-on-one, trauma-informed psychotherapy, where I learned that I did not have to keep living in fear or accepting pain as normal. (Thank you, Ms.

Lisa!) Therapy taught me how to live differently. It helped me to rewire my brain. To unlearn what I once assumed was love, and relearn what it truly means to feel safe, seen, and whole. The turning point came when I began listening to how I felt. Not how I was told to feel. Not what others assumed I should feel. But what I wanted. What I needed. And what was true about me.

The trauma I experienced was not my fault. But healing? That was my responsibility. I had to respond to what was rising within me. I wanted more than just survival. I wanted to become something. So, I chose to believe in myself, even when my ex-husband said I was not good enough. Even when he told me he would not help me with our children. Even when he swore, I would never get into The Ohio State University. But I did not allow his words to influence my heart's desire. Not only did I gain admission, but I also graduated with honors twice and earned my master's degree. Graduating with honors was proof of my resilience.

But even with those victories, healing is not a straight line.

5

THE ECHOES WITHIN

*Childhood whispers do not vanish; they
echo until someone listens.*

Healing isn't a straight line. Even as I celebrated victories, echoes of the little girl inside me still rose to the surface; the one who had learned to survive by being silent. Her memories lived in me, surfacing when I least expected. One of the loudest echoes took me back to when I was nine years old, sitting alone in a laundromat on W. Broad Street. I remember getting there early in the morning and staying until it was dark outside. What stood out the most was that my mother and I had not brought any clothes to wash. And the second thing that stood out was that I had been dropped off. My mother told me to sit in a chair in front of the counter. She walked away and never came back.

Because of my age, I was not really aware of how to tell time, let alone measure it. But after what felt like hours of sitting, I told the person behind the counter that

I needed to go to the bathroom. They pointed to the back. I got up and walked toward it, glancing around, hoping to see my mother. She was not there. When I came back, I asked for her. "She's next door," they said. So, I walked outside, turned right, and entered an open doorway. It was a little dark inside, but I still looked around for my mother until someone stopped me and yelled, "This is a bar! Get out of here, little girl!"

I quickly turned around, walked past the laundromat, and entered another open door, but there was still no sign of her. I returned to the laundromat and told the person at the counter I could not find my mom. "She'll come back," they said. "Do you want some chips?" I was a little hungry, so without hesitation, I said yes. I sat back down in the chair, eating my chips and drinking a can of Hawaiian Punch. As the sun set and people began leaving, I watched the laundromat grow empty. Eventually, even the person behind the counter started packing up to close.

"You need to wait outside for your mom," they said. It was dark outside. I was afraid. But I slowly made my way toward the front door when suddenly, an older woman rushed in and said, "I'm here to pick you up." I did not ask any questions. I did not hesitate. I just went. To this day, she is still a stranger. She never told me her name. But I assumed my mother had sent her. How else would she know I was there? How did she know my mother? Where was my mother?

I did not know the answers. I just got into her fancy

car. She talked to me kindly and told me she had been married for a long time. She said she had four children and a grandchild whose birthday party would be at her house the next day. When we pulled up to her home, not far from W. Broad Street, she parked on the opposite side of the street from the driver's seat. Then she got out, walked over to my side, opened the door, and led me up several steps to a big house with a lovely front porch with furniture. When we stepped inside, I noticed the house had a lot of glass figurines, mirrors, and panel walls. She whispered, "Shhh…my husband is sleeping. I don't want to wake him."

She took me downstairs to the lower level of her home, turned on two lamps, lit a cigarette, and lay on a high bed. I stood by the bedroom door and asked where my mom was. "She'll pick you up tomorrow," she said. "Come on, get up in this bed. I want you to do something." The smell of her cigarette. The scent of her perfume. The odor of her body. It all came rushing in as I came closer to her bed.

The two lamps, one a tall floor lamp that resembled long fingers stretching out on the right side of the bed, and the other a large lamp on the left side of the bed, sat on a nightstand. The window was on the right side of the room. She had long arms and legs, long fingers covered with rings. It seemed my mind began taking pictures as I noticed every detail of the woman and everything that surrounded me. She helped me up onto her bed. She had on a loose-fitted dress that she began taking off. The older woman didn't have any underclothes on. Her breasts were smaller than my mother's, and her pubic hair was whitish-gray. She pulled me nearer and asked me to touch her breast. Her breasts were so soft to me. The woman, who was also a grandmother, told me to do things that made me feel like life couldn't be more evil than this.

The next day, just like the woman said, my mother picked me up. I did not even get to stay for the birthday party. My mother and the woman whispered in another room, but I was not privy to their conversation. I just stood there waiting and watching. My gut tells me my mother knew about the sexual assault. And if she knew, and did not say anything, she was in on it.

Being exposed to sexual abuse from such an early age and throughout my childhood, by countless people, felt normal. So many people touched me: young, old, men, women, family, strangers—and my mother—their violations can never be undone.

- The images.
- The smells.
- The violations.
- The words.
- The feelings.

It was painful to experience. It was isolating. It was deeply depressing. And it did not just affect my physical body, it altered my mind,

my spirit, my soul. It shaped my self-esteem, my confidence, and my understanding of what beauty was. It shaped how I walked and how I talked. It shaped my future, long before I could ever see it. It shaped how I thought I would be as a woman. How I would be as a wife and one day parent. It shaped how I viewed God and what life was all about.

The molestation, the rape, the exploitation, the threats of death, the near-death experiences, all of it shaped how I would show up for myself, and how I would one day show up for my children or lack thereof.

It is a profound betrayal when adults sexually violate, physically abuse, and verbally shame children. It shatters children's trust in the very people meant to protect them. When children are violated, abused, and shamed, it creates a narrative, one that is stitched together with fear, pain, and silence.

Without awareness, that narrative doesn't go away. It lingers. It lives inside the mind, body, and soul of an innocent child who is unspoken but present. It weaves itself into the very fabric of their being. It becomes a silent ache, a sorrow that shapes how they think, feel, and see themselves.

Always searching for a way to be heard. To be witnessed. To be named. There is no magic eraser that removes abuse. Just because a child does not share their story does not mean there isn't one. And it certainly does not mean it did not bother them or that it does not affect them. On the contrary, it bothered them, and it shaped how they present and show up for themselves. Left un-spoken, that pain does not fade: it grows roots. But when we dare to name it, we begin the process of loosening those roots and reclaiming our ground.

6

CONDITIONED TO FEAR AND KEEP SILENT

*Fear disguised as love teaches silence
until truth finds its voice.*

Those roots show up in the body, in the heart, in how a child learns to trust or not trust the world around them. In my earliest years, fear began when no one came to comfort me. Had someone responded to my cries consistently as an infant or gently held me as a toddler, I wonder if I would have said something to an adult about being sexually abused when I was a little girl. But the painful truth is that I was not seen enough for anyone to ask, "Are you okay?" or "Are you safe?"

I was a neglected infant, left to cry without comfort, held without tenderness, and passed between people who did not see me. That experience shaped my emotional understanding of the world. Without language, my body learned this truth: No one is coming even if I cry loudly.

Because no one ever did, and if they did come, they did not stay.

As I grew older, the neglect continued and eventually became sexual, physical, and emotional abuse layered over years of poverty, and a mother caught in her addiction. I was not taught that what I was experiencing was abuse. I was not taught that it was wrong. But my body knew. And my amygdala knew.

The body is always listening. It remembers what the

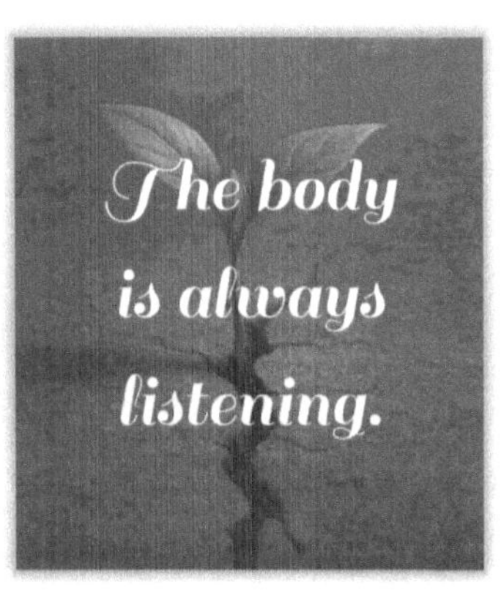

mind cannot process. As trauma expert Bessel van der Kolk (2014) explains, "the body keeps the score," holding the imprints of trauma in muscles, breath, and nervous system patterns long after the events are over. My nervous system learned early that the world was not safe, that people who should protect you can also hurt you, and that crying would not bring comfort. Those lessons were not spoken out loud, but they were etched into my body like unshakable truths.

I grew up on high alert, constantly scanning for danger. I did not know that what I felt was hyper-vigilance; I just knew that my chest tightened when someone's voice got too loud and that my stomach dropped when footsteps came too close. My body braced itself for impact, even when there was none. I was living in survival mode, long before I even knew what survival mode was. Fear became the lens through which I saw everything; relationships, love, and safety. I did not have the language for boundaries or trust. All I knew was how to endure, to stay small, and to keep the peace by silencing myself. This was not living; it was surviving on instincts, instincts that were wired by neglect and sharpened by abuse.

My amygdala, the brain's alarm system, stored every scream, every inappropriate touch, every bruise, and every moment of terror as proof that I needed to stay on guard. Neuroscientists like Joseph LeDoux (1996) describe the amygdala as central to fear learning, storing emotional memories and sounding the alarm long after the danger has passed. It doesn't care about love or joy; its only job is to keep me alive. And when your nervous system is built on survival, safety feels like a foreign language, and love often feels like fear.

I was not taught what safe love looked like. No one showed me how it felt to be nurtured, to be comforted, to be held without harm. Instead, I learned that silence kept the peace and that staying small kept me from getting hurt. When love is mixed with fear, a child learns to accept even the smallest scraps of kindness as something to hold onto. That confusion followed me. As I grew older, I confused control with care, attention with affection, and pain with love. My body responded to danger as if it were familiar, as if it belonged. The echoes of my childhood whispered that love was supposed to hurt. That safety wasn't absolute; only fleeting moments between storms.

By the time I was a young woman, I did not recognize the difference between love and fear. My body was conditioned to see them as one. I found myself drawn to what felt familiar, not realizing that familiarity was not safety; it was just unhealed wounds disguised as comfort. My nervous system craved what it knew, even when what it knew was harmful. So, when I met my first husband, who mirrored the unpredictability of my childhood, I stayed. I stayed even when it hurt, believing that leaving meant I had failed, or maybe I just was not good enough to make our marriage last. I had been taught: Love was something to endure, not something that would nurture or protect.

Love was something to endure, not something that would nurture.

This is how abuse continues its cycle. It teaches us to settle for pain, to mistake fear for passion, and to silence ourselves in the hope that love will finally come if we hold on long enough. I did not yet understand that the love I was looking for would never come from someone else; it had to start with me. But I was too lost, too conditioned, to see that truth at the time.

It took years before I realized that what I had accepted as love was the absence of it. Therapy became the mirror I never had, reflecting the truth that my silence was not strength; it was survival. I learned to name what had been unnamed for so long: neglect, abuse, fear. Saying those words out loud felt like pulling stones from my chest, one by one.

Faith carried me when the weight of it all felt too heavy. I began to believe that God did not create me to live in fear or to be broken down by someone else's pain. He created me to be whole, to be free, and to stand in the fullness of who I am. That belief gave me the courage to keep going when I wanted to retreat, to trust that healing was possible even when it felt out of reach.

Self-awareness came slowly, but once it arrived, I could no longer ignore the truth. I started to see the patterns. Every time I silenced myself, I repeated what I had learned as a child. I began to challenge those old lessons, to question the belief that I had to accept pain to feel loved. It was not easy, but every step toward awareness was a step away from the fear that once controlled me.

Healing did not erase the fear but taught me to face it.

To see where it started, how it shaped me, and why I kept calling fear "love." It showed me that I was never broken, only conditioned.

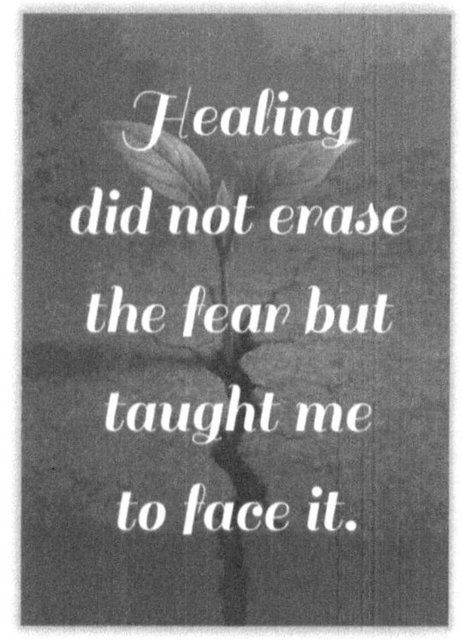

That safety was not something I had to earn through silence or suffering. It was something I had always deserved. And while my body had learned to survive, my spirit longed to speak. To name the truth. To finally confront the illusion that what was done to me did not matter, did not last, or did not leave scars. Because it did. And no matter how much time has passed, I remember. Not just in my mind, but in my body, my breath, and in the deepest parts of me. The fear I carried as a child never disappeared. It echoed quietly inside me, shaping how I trusted, loved, and saw myself.

— 7 —

THE MYTH OF FORGETTING

The body never forgets what the mind
tries to erase.

Even as I began to heal, I could not help but wonder: did the people who caused this pain ever think about what they left behind? Do abusers believe the pain they inflicted disappears? Do they convince themselves we imagined it all, that the sexual abuse, the rough hands, the whispered threats, and the unbearable shame were fragments of a child's imagination? Do they think our memories dissolved with time? That fear was washed away like dirt after a long day. That we simply grew up and "got over it." Or do they think we possess some superpower, some unexplainable magic that allows us to shake off trauma as if it never happened?

And do perpetrators of domestic violence and sexual assault believe that the threats, the manipulation, the control, and the gaslighting will be forgotten? Do they imagine that the bruises that faded from our skin disappeared from our memory? That our broken bones healed, therefore we are healed? Or that the rage in their eyes, the isolation tactics, the slammed doors, the nights we cried ourselves to sleep were just emotional overreactions?

Do they think we no longer flinch when voices are raised? Do they think we no longer feel our stomachs drop when someone's footsteps sound too heavy? Do they believe trauma simply evaporates once we leave or once they mutter, "Sorry?"

Here's what they fail to imagine:

- The child grows up.
- The victim becomes a survivor.
- And the survivor may be inspired to share their lived experience.

Abusers should think longer and harder before creating victims, because one day, those victims may write. We will give voice to the silence we were forced to carry. And the abuser will not be forgotten. We remember their facial expressions. Their voice. Their stance. Their scent. Because when you are terrified, your senses record everything. The roughness of their hands. The wrinkles in their skin. The details of a tattoo. The coarseness of a beard. Fear is a camera. Trauma is a film.

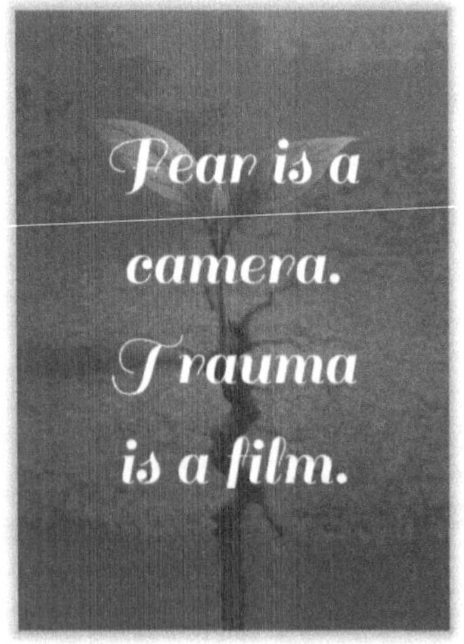

Abusers may pretend it didn't happen. They may hope we forget. But neuroscience says otherwise. As trauma expert Bessel van der Kolk (2014) explains, the brain doesn't store trauma like ordinary memories. Instead, the body remembers through the amygdala, the brain's fear center, which records every detail during moments of terror. Neuroscientist Joseph LeDoux (1996) describes this same process in *The Emotional Brain*, showing how the amygdala imprints fear memories with striking precision, even when the conscious mind cannot recall them. That is why I remember their voice, their smell, and the weight of their silence. My body held onto what they wanted me to forget.

Abusers do not consider that the child they hurt becomes an adult who still remembers everything. An adult who might fall into another abuser's hands, not because they "chose" pain, but because their body was wired to normalize it. Perpetrators do not think about how their abuse created patterns. They do not see that the survival skills an adult learned as a child—numbing, shrinking, pleasing—were the same skills that kept them in a violent marriage. Cycles that were named and patterns that had to be broken.

For years, I did not speak about what my mother did to me as a child. I did not talk about what my ex-husband did to me as a woman. But why? My silence was not just about fear; it was about the conditioning of secrecy. I was taught in childhood to accept abuse and keep it a secret. Those early scripts shaped how I stayed, how I endured, and how I believed suffering was normal even in my adulthood. No more. Not for revenge, but because my experience is mine to tell, and my healing is mine to live.

But speaking my truth did not come easily.

AWAKENING MY VOICE

When one of us rises, we remind others
that rising is possible.
—Amanda D. Ligon

THE COURAGE TO SPEAK

*Healing begins the moment silence loses
its grip on your voice.*

Silence had been planted in me as a child, teaching me that compliance meant safety and loyalty meant keeping quiet. I wore silence like skin, breathing it in as if it were protection. Fear felt familiar, almost like home, my normal. By the time I was a woman, that conditioning had taken root so deeply that I mistook suffering for loyalty and wounds for proof of love. But a home built on fear is not a place to live; it is a place to escape.

When fear becomes the language you grow up speaking, it takes years to learn a new one. I stayed where I was hurting, not because I did not know I was hurting, but because I thought that is what love required. To forgive endlessly, to keep trying, and to prove I was worthy enough to make someone stay. My nervous system had memorized fear, shame, and chaos, like old lullabies sung over and over. It did not know how to rest in peace or safety.

No one tells you that when you grow up in abuse, your body learns to normalize what should never feel normal. I did not just tolerate fear; I expected it. I was wired to believe that something was wrong with me if I was not in fear, or that love was not real unless it left scars. It is a deep lie that seeps into every part of your life; into your choices, your relationships, and the way you see yourself in the mirror.

Even though I was suffering, my nervous system was learning: "This is how you survive. This is what love must be." Psychologists have long studied how our behaviors are shaped by reinforcement. B.F. Skinner (1938) described this as operant conditioning, the way behavior continues when it is reinforced by either reward or relief.

There are two kinds of reinforcement:

- Positive Reinforcement – something added to increase behavior
  (praise, gifts, approval)
- Negative Reinforcement – something removed to increase behavior
  (avoiding punishment, pain relief)

In traumatic situations, conditioning is not always obvious. I learned that staying silent often kept me safer than speaking up. Compliance meant less chaos. So, I complied. Not needing anything meant I would not be punished. So, I stopped needing. And these patterns became embedded in me, not as conscious choices, but as survival blueprints. Even though my mother abused me,

I stayed connected to her, because I had been wired from a young age to believe that her needs mattered more than mine. That I was supposed to help her. That my fear had to serve a purpose, her comfort.

When I met my first husband, I did not see the red flags for what they were. His anger did not shock me. His control did not feel foreign. It felt like something my body already knew. I had been conditioned to believe that if I loved hard enough, forgave enough, or made myself small enough, things would get better. I did not see that I was not being loved, I was being broken down in familiar ways.

Abuse doesn't always initially come in with fists raised. Sometimes it comes with charm, apologies, and promises to change. I knew that pattern because I had lived it as a child. I believed that if I stayed long enough, my love would fix him. The same way I once believed that my mother's protection would come if I were good enough.

That is how I learned to mistake fear for love. I thought love meant tolerating pain, waiting for the good moments to come, and proving my worth by staying. No matter how much it hurt. That was the script written into me as a child, and I carried it with

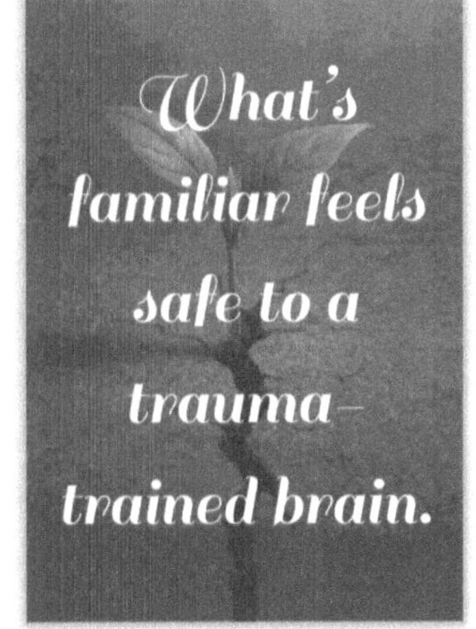

me into adulthood without even realizing it.

I did not accept abuse in my first marriage because I didn't know it was abuse. I accepted it because it felt familiar, and what's familiar feels safe to a trauma-trained brain. My husband told me over and over:

- "You're ugly."
- "You're worthless."
- "No one wants you."
- "You're f'd up from your childhood."

Unfortunately, I believed what he would say about me; so, I accepted his words as truth. In reality, those were not just his words; they were echoes of my childhood. And every time I stayed silent, did not argue, did not leave, the cycle got reinforced. Not just by fear, but by:

- Being told I was lucky to be a housewife.
- Having everything I wanted materially.
- Being praised during the honeymoon phase.
- The illusion of a "family"—Mom, Dad, and children under one roof.

Even though my body was breaking, my trauma-trained brain kept saying, "This is what love looks like. This is how you survive." I have learned that reinforcement does not always come with clapping or cheering. Sometimes, reinforcement looks like:

- Having a roof over your head.
- No disconnect notice of utilities.
- Food to feed your children.
- A car in the driveway.

And having these needs met kept me tied to a cycle of being unloved. It was less painful than usual. What I did not know then was that I was caught in something psychologists call trauma bonding—a pattern where abuse is paired with intermittent kindness, apology, or relief. This inconsistency creates a deep psychological attachment that mimics love but is built on survival instincts. As Patrick Carnes (1997) explains, "The trauma bond is stronger when the victim is dependent on the abuser emotionally, financially, or physically." Intermittent reinforcement is the most potent kind, the same principle that drives gambling and addiction. You hold on, not because of what is happening in the moment, but because of what might happen next.

- Maybe they will change.
- Perhaps they will learn to love me.
- Maybe it will be different tomorrow.

Breaking the conditioning and beginning my healing did not start with bravery; it started with awareness. When a therapist told me, "There is nothing wrong with you. You are in a domestic violence relationship," that truth created a crack in the lie. And healing slipped in through that crack.

The local church taught me to pray, journal, cry, and reflect. My body began to feel sensations it had previously numbed. And I slowly began to unlearn what had once conditioned me to stay and believe it was normal. I discovered:

- I was not F'd up.

- I was not weak.
- I was not broken.
- I was not the problem.
- I was not to blame.
- I was conditioned!

I was conditioned to believe fear was love. Conditioned to serve, submit, and silence myself. Conditioned to accept crumbs and call them blessings. I had to unlearn that I am not my conditioning. I learned to choose differently. I learned to rewrite the patterns that once defined me.

And that rewriting began with truth.

For so long, I carried the silence of what had been done to me as a child, as a wife, as a mother, believing it was my job to protect everyone else's comfort. But silence is its own kind of prison. It binds you to fear. It makes you believe the lie that your voice will only make things worse. The truth is the moment I began to speak was when the chains started to break. But truth has a way of echoing back through time, calling me to remember where the silence first cost me the most.

—9—

THE BEGINNING OF HEALING

Healing taught me that freedom begins with truth. But truth carries echoes. The body remembers what the mind tries to forget, and sometimes the past calls me back, not to harm me, but to help me understand the roots of my pain.

And the truth was this: I was young, pregnant, and recently married when the first blow landed, the first slap, the first threat that stole my breath. I wanted to believe it was a mistake, a moment of anger he did not mean. But the mark on my face, the sting on my cheek, told a different story. A voice deep inside whispered, "If he loves you, it should not feel like this." That voice was not loud yet, but it was steady. It told me that if I stayed silent, this moment would only be the beginning of something worse.

Honestly, I did not know what to do. So, I left, not for

good, but just for the night. I took my four-year-old son, and we slept in my car. He was not afraid. He was smiling the next morning, wrapped in his Mickey Mouse comforter, excited to have McDonald's for breakfast.

I was a young wife who had been taught to endure, submit, and keep the family together no matter what. The world teaches women that leaving is failure, and I was terrified of failing. So, as the sun rose, I wiped my face, smiled back at my son, and convinced myself that I could make this work. I did not know then that my silence, my return, would train my body to tolerate pain, to swallow the truth.

I did not realize the message my silence was planting in my son's nervous system. I was not aware that his tiny neurons were firing, forming a story inside him—one that would settle beneath his Mickey Mouse comforter. I never stopped to ask what he might have been feeling or thinking as we left in the middle of the night to sleep in my car.

Not even six months later, still pregnant, I left again. Another night. Another escape. With my four-year-old son in tow. This time, I called Rena, whom I had known since I was fifteen. She had taken me in when I was eighteen and had nowhere to go. Now I am eight months pregnant. Still newly married. Still enduring slaps, intimidation, threats, and name-calling from my first husband.

And again, I had no thought of what my son was carrying. What it meant to leave our home in the dark. What it meant to watch a man, his stepfather, straddle his pregnant mother. To witness his mother pregnant and powerless to stop it. Or to be thrown by his stepfather, by his face into his bed.

For years, I held this pain and shame in silence. Survivors are often told to protect the person who hurt them, told not to speak, told not to ruin someone else's reputation, said that to tell the truth is to betray. To talk about what happened is to bring shame. Not to the abuser, but to yourself. But no one asks: What did it cost you to stay silent? What did it do to your body, your children, your sense of self?

Secrets do not protect the abused. They protect the abuser. And I carried that secret like a second skin. Until I could not anymore. Telling my story was an act of liberation. The day I told the truth; I did not betray anyone. I stopped betraying myself. Releasing the secret did not come from a place of revenge. It came from a place of reclamation. A need to be seen. To be heard. To be free. I was not speaking to hurt anyone. I was talking because the silence was hurting me.

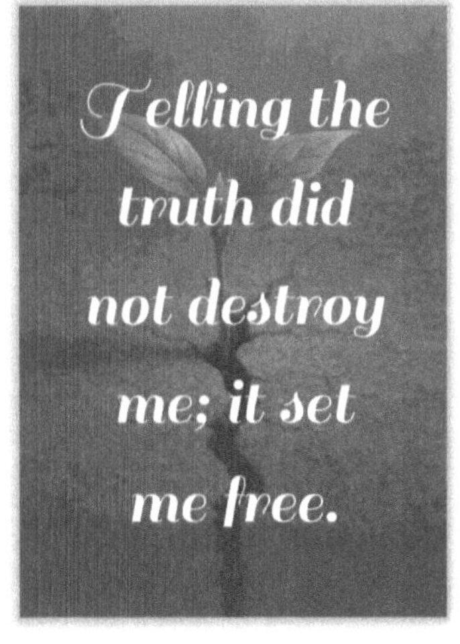

My silence did not just keep my suffering a secret. It taught my children to be quiet. It taught them to live on edge and to be defensive. Unsure if their father would be angry with me or if I would be walking on pins and needles, trying not to upset him. That is not a healthy childhood. That is a battlefield.

Had I known the lasting effects of my silence–the way it would echo into my children's lives, shaping their fears, stealing their voices, and robbing them of their innocence–I would have stayed gone the first time I left. I would have chosen differently, not just for me, but for them. But I did not know. I only knew fear, pain, tears, and living in secrecy.

The first time my son felt fear, the first time I was struck while pregnant, should have been enough to make me leave for good. Yet I was conditioned to stay, to keep silent, and to accept the violations as normal.

But I see it now. Silence was never protection; it was prison. Secrets did not shield me, they shackled me. And every moment I hushed my truth, the cost only grew heavier, spilling into my body and my children's lives. Breaking that silence was where healing began. It was the moment I stopped carrying everyone else's shame and I began reclaiming my own voice.

PART FOUR

TRANSFORMATION

You do not have to get over it—
you have to go through it.
—Amanda D. Ligon

10

ENDING THE CYCLES

*Cycles end when one heart dares to
choose differently.*

When I think of my older children, I remember when I was not conscious of breaking cycles. I was trying to survive. I mothered them from my wounds, protecting them with the only tools I had; silence, instinct, and the deep ache of knowing I did not want them to feel what I had felt as a child. I did not have the language for trauma or healing then; I only knew I wanted to love them differently than I had been loved, even if I did not always know how.

But looking back now, I see the difference in how I mothered my younger children. When they became of age that they started asking, "Mommy, are you okay?" I refused to let them grow up in a home filled with the same cycle of domestic violence that their older siblings had witnessed. My survival had turned into intention. I had learned to recognize the cycles I was in, and I made a choice: the cycle would not continue.

Breaking the cycle did not happen overnight. It did not happen the first time I left, the second, or even the fifth. It was a slow awakening. A painful process of realizing that I was not just surviving anymore. I was raising children who were learning to survive, too.

It was not until I had my fourth child that I truly saw it. Another son. Another daughter. And yet, the same cycle of physical abuse, sexual violations, and mind games. It felt like déjà vu, as if I had dragged another generation of children into the same dark room I kept trying to escape.

I will never forget the night my youngest son busted open the bedroom door because he heard his father threatening me. He heard my cries, his mother pleading and begging to be released. That moment, something split open in me. I saw myself through his terrified eyes, and I knew: this was not the home I wanted to raise two more children in.

I had to convince myself that being a stay-at-home wife and having their father in the home was not worth my children's well-being. Here I was, stuck in the very cycle I swore I would break. And leaving was not enough, I had to relocate out of state to break the cycle of domestic violence.

The journey to breaking the cycle was not just about escaping abuse. It was about learning to name it. I only knew pain. I only knew survival. I only knew what I saw and experienced. And I did not have the language to call it what it was for years. I did not know my entire life had been shaped by abuse behind closed doors.

Healing from my childhood meant facing truths I had buried deep, truths about my mother's hands that harmed instead of held, her words that cut instead of comforted. For years, I carried her pain inside me, thinking it was mine to bear. But I made a vow, even before I had words for it, that I would not become what broke me. I would not numb my pain with drugs or alcohol. I would not use my hands or my silence to harm my children. I would not make them pay for what I survived.

Healing for me meant parenting from gentleness, not pain. It meant choosing softness when my body remembered hardness, demonstrating love when I was hurting. It was breathing through frustration instead of letting it spill over. It also meant apologizing when I got it wrong. Every time I chose calm over chaos, I was rewriting my story. I was teaching my children what safety feels like.

My healing became my resistance. Every hug, every boundary, every prayer over my children was a quiet rebellion against everything I was taught love should be. I did not just break the cycle by leaving an abuse. I broke it by becoming the kind of mother I never had. And that, to me, is the truest healing of all.

Yet healing doesn't erase the past. It asks you to face it differently to understand how it shaped you. Only then did I begin to see the pattern clearly enough to break it. That's where my real work began.

From my earliest memory, I was abused physically,

emotionally, and sexually. I was neglected, ignored, and betrayed. I asked my mother to kill me when I was in elementary school. I attempted suicide in high school. My mother was my sexual predator, and for over 20 years, I was married to a man who raped me, beat up on me, and degraded me constantly. And still I never inflicted my pain on my children.

Why?

Some might say it is because I am strong. But the truth is more complicated. Because the heartbreaking reality is that many who survive abuse repeat their pain. Many become what they once despised. Not out of malice, but because pain unprocessed becomes pain passed on.

Let me be clear: abuse does not automatically create abusers. But unprocessed trauma, unmet needs, and a dysregulated nervous system can build a cycle of harm. Especially when there is no intervention, safety, or one modeling a different way of being. I did not break the cycle by accident. And it was not because I was fearless or knew exactly what I was doing, because I did not. I broke it one trembling step at a time, stumbling, often returning, before I finally found the strength to stay gone.

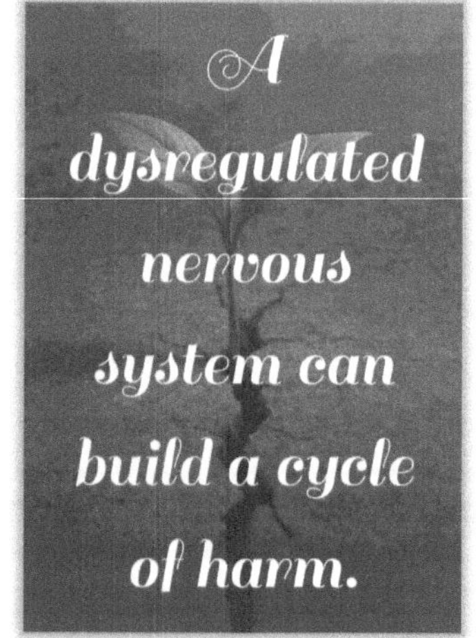

For years, I thought staying in my marriage meant protecting my children. I told myself that having both parents under one roof was better than raising them without their father in the home. I had convinced myself that enduring the abuse was worth it if it meant they would not grow up without a father. I told myself lies, I did not even know were lies, because no one had ever taught me the difference between love and control, between family and captivity.

But deep down, I started to notice what my silence was costing our children. They were learning the same hyper-vigilance I grew up with. I saw my older children watching my body language like I used to watch my mother. Scanning for signs that something was wrong. I saw them trying to manage my moods or soften their father's temper, taking on burdens no child should carry.

It hit me: *I was raising survivors, not children. And I didn't want that to be their story.*

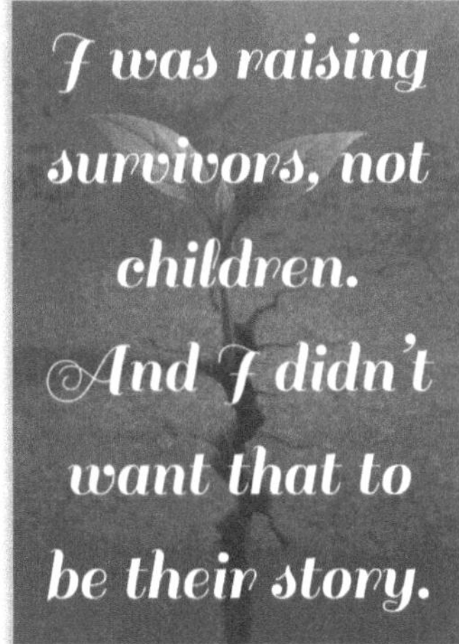

For me, leaving was terrifying because staying had become my "normal." I was conditioned from childhood to believe that you earned love by enduring pain. So, I stayed. I stayed until I saw my children flinching at raised voices. I stayed until I reflected on my youngest son busting through that bedroom door, was a cry for his mother, who would fight for them. Even if it meant losing everything else.

That was the day I began to leave for real, not just physically but emotionally. I started to detach from the illusion of *family* I had been clinging to. I started imagining a future where my children could grow up peacefully.

Leaving abuse is hard, but staying gone feels nearly impossible when you have been conditioned to return. But my faith helped me stay gone. Every time I doubted myself, I prayed. Every time I felt like I might fall apart, I opened my journal and poured out my soul. Whenever I was tempted to go back to the pain, I was so familiar with, I whispered, "God, remind me why I left." Even when I did not have the words to say, I moaned in prayer. Prayer became my refuge when I felt trapped in silence. It was where I learned to exhale the pain I could not tell anyone else about. In prayer, I felt seen by God, even when I felt invisible to the world.

I did not know anything about neuroscience then, but I now understand that prayer, worship, and stillness were regulating my nervous system. Research has shown that contemplative prayer and meditation activate the parasympathetic nervous system, lowering stress and increasing a sense of peace (Newberg & Waldman, 2009). These spiritual practices created small moments of safety that rewired my brain, even amid chaos.

The more I prayed, the stronger I became. The stronger I became, the more I believed I can do all things through Christ that strengthens me (Philippians 4:13). I was less tempted to go back when I began to see myself through God's eyes: worthy, loved, and capable. And slowly, I started to believe that my children and I were meant for more than fear.

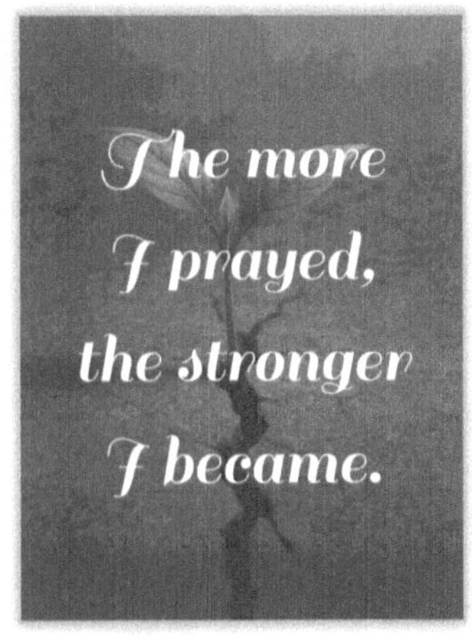

After breaking cycles and actually naming it, I discovered the need to rebuild my mind, body, and spirit so that I wouldn't return to or connect with that kind of pain again.

What also helped me were not grand gestures or heroic rescues. It was small, sacred interventions of hope. Tiny moments of safety and care that whispered to my nervous system, "Life can be different than this."

As a little girl, I sometimes spent the night at my Uncle Connie and Aunt Rita's house. Back then, I did not have the language for it, but those visits gave me something my home did not: structure, calm, and consistency. I remember the smell of food cooking on the stove, cereal stored in Tupperware on top of the refrigerator, and the quiet hum of the television with cable. Something I did not have at home. Their home felt like peace. It planted a seed deep inside me saying, "This is what safety feels like." And I created a home that I remembered my uncle and aunt had.

Later, as a teenager, I met Rena, a Teenage Prevention Specialist at Sawyer Recreation Center. I had no idea at the time how much she would impact my life. She did not save me in an obvious way, but she modeled something I had never seen up close: a woman standing tall, working with purpose, and creating change in her community. She showed me that women could be powerful, kind, strong, and compassionate without saying a word. My nervous system took note, even when my mind did not fully understand. So, I became the woman Rena modeled in front of me.

These moments might have seemed small, even forgettable, to someone else. But to me, they were proof that another way of living existed. They proved that chaos was not the only language a family could speak.

I have realized how much the presence of safe people could shape my healing. I met countless amazing friends who saw me, not just the pain I carried, but the strength I did not even know I had. Many prayed with me. Some sat with me. Others shared meals, conversations, or a quiet understanding that I was not alone. Research calls this co-regulation—how our nervous system calms when we are with someone who feels safe and sees us without judgment (Porges, 2011; Schore, 2003). But I call it grace.

Grace, that amid my pain, I had micro-moments with

people that opened their heart and showed me kindness. It was through these relationships that gave me a glimmer of what I could have and become. Experiencing safe connections told my body:

- You are safe.
- You are not broken.
- You are not what they did to you.
- You are worthy of love and peace.

Breaking the cycle was not just about what I walked away from. It was about who I became on the other side. I learned that resilience is not about being tough or pretending nothing hurts. Resilience is the quiet rebellion of choosing to heal. It is saying, "You may have harmed me, but I refuse to carry your harm forward."

Ending the cycle of abuse was not a single act of bravery. It was a thousand small choices, made in the dark, with trembling hands and a heart that refused to stop beating for my children. It was the night I finally said, "No more." It was every moment I chose prayer over despair, faith over fear, and healing over silence.

I know now that God was with me in every step, even when I was a child and felt utterly alone. God was with me in the quiet nights when I held my children close and prayed for a better tomorrow. God was with me when I packed up my life, moved out of state, and did not know the freeway from my house. And God was with me when I decided that I would never again call pain "home."

The cycle ends with me.

I say that not as a badge of perfection, but as a testament to grace. My children are not growing up in the shadow of my silence anymore. They are growing up with a mother who speaks, chooses peace, and knows

that love does not come with bruises or fear. What was meant to break me has built me. What was meant to silence me has given me a voice. What was meant for evil, God turned for my good. And every day I wake up, I am living proof that the cycle of fear and pain is broken.

But breaking free was only the beginning.

11

TO HEAL DEEPLY

*To heal deeply is to become whole; not
in spite of the pain, but through it.*

Leaving the abuse didn't erase the pain. It gave me space to feel it. For years, I had ignored myself by serving others to survive. I stuffed down my emotions because I believed that if I let them rise, they would swallow me whole. But healing requires more than walking away. It requires turning to what hurts you and truly feeling it: every memory, every ache, every unspoken word. It is not easy to face what you have spent a lifetime running from. But I learned you cannot heal what you refuse to feel.

That is what I began to discover next: the courage to feel it all so I could finally, heal deeply.

For most of my life, I believed that ignoring the pain made me stronger. I thought if I kept moving, smiling, and surviving, then maybe I could outrun what had been done to me. I learned early on that showing emotion was dangerous. Tears could be mocked, screams could be silenced, and anger could lead to more punishment. So, I buried it all.

But what I did not realize was that the pain I buried did not disappear. It lived inside me, quietly shaping the way I breathed, the way I slept, the way I loved and trusted. It was in my muscles, always tight. In my jaw, always clenched. In the pit of my stomach, always on guard. Trauma does not leave just because we stop talking about it. It lingers in the body like smoke after a fire.

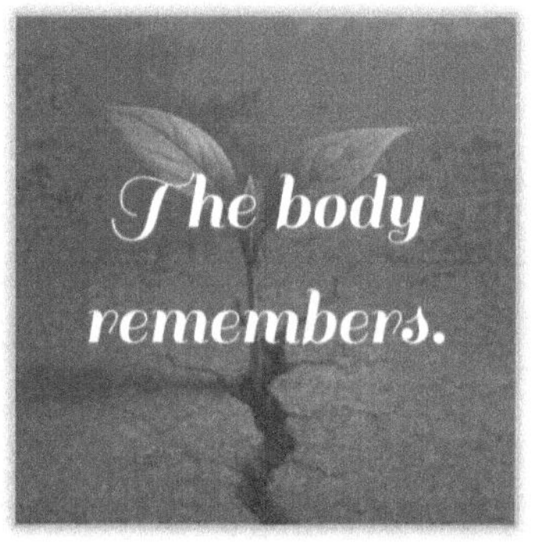

The body remembers.

Even when the mind tries to forget, the body holds the truth. My nervous system had been on high alert for so long that I did not know what safety felt like. I mistook numbness for peace. I confused silence with healing. And I did not understand that to heal truly, I had to acknowledge my feelings. Not just the pain of my past, but the weight of all the years I had carried it. Feeling fully was terrifying at first. It felt like opening a floodgate I was not sure I could control. But every time I allowed myself to cry, to grieve, to rage in healthy ways, I was reclaiming pieces of myself I had long abandoned.

As I began to face my pain, I realized that my body had been speaking to me all along. Long before I understood words like abuse or infection, my body was carrying the weight of it. I remember the burning that started in my vagina when I was a little girl. An unbearable burning that made it hard to sit in class, to walk, to simply be. I remember the shame of the odor, the fidgeting, and the desperate attempts to soothe myself. From as early as elementary school, I had learned to self-medicate. Not with pills or potions–but with cold baths, baby powder, and Vaseline when it was there. It was through trial and error that I learned not to use rubbing alcohol and always to wash my hands before I applied my homemade remedies. I did what I could. I did not have the language to say, "I'm hurting." I did not even know what was wrong. But my body knew. It was holding what I could not speak.

No one asked why I always squirmed in my chair or stayed quiet, never raising my hand. No one noticed the silent war for healing being fought within me. I learned to push through, to smile on the outside while my body screamed in pain. Yet I thought this was normal because that burning had been with me since my earliest childhood until early high school.

Now, I understand that my body was not betraying me; it was warning me. It was trying to tell me that something was deeply wrong. My body became the messenger of what I could not yet name: the harm I was living through, and the infections that came from it. It spoke the truth I could not say out loud. Every ache, every sting, every restless night was my body's way of whispering, "You are being hurt, and you need help."

There came a point when I could no longer silence my body's voice. The same body that once burned, ached, and trembled in fear began to ache in new ways as I got older, through anxiety, tension, exhaustion, and deep sadness that no homemade remedies could cure. My body remembered everything I had tried to forget. It carried the echoes of every "don't tell," every flinch, every moment I was forced to be still when I wanted to run. For so long, I thought something was wrong with me. But in truth, something had happened to me. My body was still trying to process what my mind had buried. The headaches, the panic, the sudden tears that came without warning, the longing to be comforted—they were not weakness or instability. They were messages. My body was asking to be heard, to finally release what it had held for far too long.

It was not until adulthood, during my healing journey, that I realized the importance of listening to my body. All the emotions I thought I had buried—fear, rage, grief—had never really gone away. They had been stored in my nervous system, connective tissues, breath, and heartbeat.

To heal, I had to release tears.

That meant crying the tears I never cried as a child. It meant sitting with

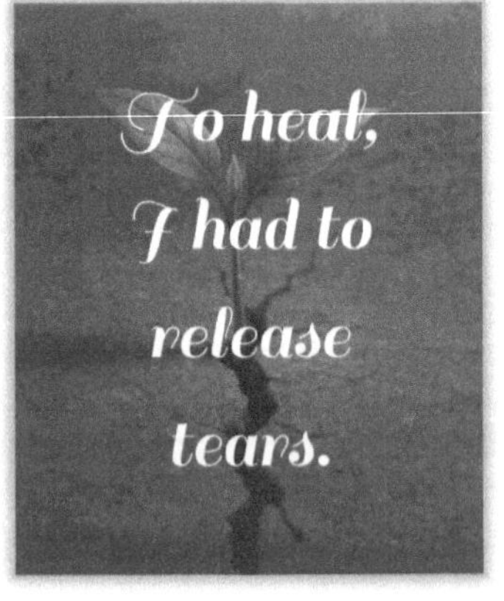

the discomfort I had always tried to numb. It meant giving my body the compassion it never received back then.

I did not know what safety felt like for most of my life. Not in my body, not in my home, not even in my thoughts. But healing taught me that you do not find safety "out there." It is something you slowly build within.

I had to learn to calm my body before I could even begin to calm my mind. That is when I discovered small, sacred practices that helped me return to myself. Practices that whispered, "You don't have to brace anymore."

I began with small practices to regulate my nervous system.

- *Breathwork*: I started with the simplest act of all—breathing. I would sit quietly and inhale deeply for four seconds, then exhale slowly for six. It was not just about oxygen; it was about telling my body, "We are not in danger anymore. We can slow down" (Jerath, Edry, Barnes, & Jerath, 2006).
- *Herbal Bath Soaks*: My bathtub became a place of renewal. I began creating herbal blends: Epsom salt for tension, rose petals for softness, chamomile, and jasmine for calm. As I sank into the warm water, I imagined all the fear and pain dissolving, leaving me lighter.
- *Journaling After My Soaks*: After my baths, I would journal whatever rose to the surface:

memories, emotions, truths I had once buried. I did not write to analyze or judge myself. I wrote to release.

- *Music*: Gentle horn melodies or the sound of rain became my companions. Music helped shift my energy, reminding me that peace had a rhythm, too.
- *Affirmations*: I learned to speak kindly to myself, something I had never heard. I would place a hand on my heart and say,
  - "You are safe now."
  - "You are not invisible."
  - "You are loved."

These were not just practices. They were acts of reclamation. Each practice told my body, "You are worthy. You are here. You are free."

I used to think healing had to be dramatic, like some big, sudden breakthrough. But now I know, it is in the quiet moments. It is in the breath I didn't have to hold. It is how my shoulders soften when I step into a warm bath. It is in the slow return of trust, not in anyone else but myself.

My nervous system, once wired only for survival, is now learning a new language: peace. And for the first time in my life, peace feels familiar.

Healing is not about pretending the pain never happened. It is not about erasing the memories or forcing myself to "get over it." Healing, I have learned, is about feeling fully. Allowing every buried emotion, every hidden ache, to rise to the surface so it can finally be seen, heard, and released.

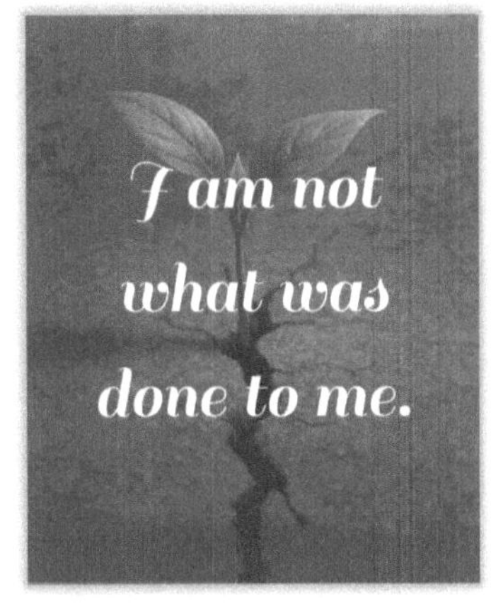

There was a time when I feared my pain would swallow me whole if I let myself feel it. But I see now that my pain was never here to destroy me. It was here to guide me. Every tear I have cried, every truth I have spoken, every breath I have taken in moments of stillness has been an act of coming home to myself.

Today, I know this: I am not my pain, my past, or what they did to me. I am the woman who faced it all, felt it all, and found healing on the other side. And the deeper I allow myself to feel, the deeper I heal.

Fully feeling and deeply healing teaches you that you were never too much. You were carrying too much pain. It shows you that love does not have to hurt, and safety is not something you have to earn. When you feel fully, you allow the old wounds to rise and release, making space for peace, an inner peace that does not just soothe the surface but transforms the soul. This is where survival gives way to transformation.

When transformation happens, peace becomes your new baseline, and everything changes. You stop attracting chaos, mistaking survival for love, and apologizing for needing gentleness.

And that is **feeling fully** and **healing deeply**.

12

MY GREATEST TEACHERS

Even the ones who broke me became the
ones who taught me who I am.

The deeper I've healed, the clearer I've become. Peace has given me clarity. As I have learned to feel fully and allow my body to heal, I can look back on my life not only with pain but with perspective. I can see the lessons hidden in the fire, even from those who tried to break me. In their own twisted way, they became my greatest teachers.

People often say, "Everyone is doing the best they can." Yet my experiences with predators, rapists, abusers, and manipulators make me question that belief. Why would they harm in secret if they were genuinely doing their best? Why would they beg, threaten, or silence their victims? Why would they hide behind masks, wearing the face of Dr. Jekyll while living as Mr. Hyde? I've learned hard truths from these people. Truths I did not ask for, truths I never wanted. But I have also gained wisdom that has shaped the woman I am today.

Lessons From My Mother,

My mother taught me what love is not. Love should not come with pain, manipulation, or secrets. Her failures became a mirror, showing me how to define love more intentionally.

I learned that silence can be deadly. Her abuse taught me the importance of voice. I had to find my own and use it, no matter who it made uncomfortable.

I also learned that motherhood is sacred. By witnessing what she gave and what she withheld, I committed to pouring into my children, into myself, into my community, and into the women I serve.

Most importantly, I learned that unless someone breaks the chain, pain will continue to pass from one generation to the next. I chose to be that chain-breaker.

Lessons From My Ex-Husband,

He taught me how control could disguise itself as love. I realized that manipulation, financial control, and emotional abuse can wear the mask of care. And I learned how to unmask it.

I also discovered that freedom is worth fleeing for. I left, even when I was pregnant. I left, even when I had small children, fear gripping me like a second skin. And though I left many times, I eventually stayed gone, declaring to myself, "This is not what I was born for."

Lastly, I realized that survival is not weakness. It is sacred strength. I lived through something that tried to crush my spirit, but instead, I rose.

Lessons From Abuse Itself,

Abuse taught me to listen to my body. My body carried memories long before my words did. It spoke through my pain, my silence, my flinching, my holding of breath. Now I honor its voice.

I am convinced that I am not what happened to me. I am not broken, damaged goods, or defined by the choices of those who hurt me.

I am fully persuaded that I am not to blame. No child, no woman, no human being is ever responsible for someone else's violence or control. There is never a reason to hit, to rape, or to break another soul.

It also taught me that healing is possible, one truth, one breath, one word at a time.

Lastly, I learned that empathy, advocacy, and purpose can grow from pain. What once felt like ruins became the foundation for my calling.

Forgiveness,

And so, I forgive.

Not because they asked me to, but because I needed

to be free. I forgive them for not loving me, for not protecting me, for not honoring the sacredness of my body, and the innocence God entrusted to them when I was placed in their care.

I forgive, not because what they did was small, it was not. Their actions carved deep wounds and years of insecurities. But my healing became greater than their harm.

In the words of Jesus, I say, "Father, forgive them, for they know not what they do" (Luke 23:34, KJV). And maybe they did know. Maybe their upbringing blinded them. Perhaps they were too wounded to love me. Maybe, like Pharaoh, their hearts were hardened (Exodus 7:3, KJV).

Maybe this. Maybe that.

None of it matters now, because I have become who I was created to be, in spite of it all. What was meant for evil, God turned it for my good.

My Mission,

Having done all, I stand, not as a victim, but as a witness. A living testimony that the fire didn't consume me, it refined me. And now, it is my mission to share my story. Not because it was easy and not for revenge, but because someone else needs to know: *You can survive. You*

can heal. You can become.

Healing does not come only from understanding the past. It comes from protecting your present. Survival taught me to endure anything. Healing taught me that I do not have to. Healing also taught me a word no one ever taught me growing up:

Boundaries.

Epilogue

When I look back on the woman I used to be—the girl who sat quietly in the dark, the young mother who didn't know how to leave, the wife who prayed for the storm to stop—I see a survivor. I see a woman who carried burdens she didn't deserve and still found a way to keep breathing, loving, and showing up. Survival was only the beginning. Healing is the story I continue to experience each day.

There came a moment when I realized I didn't want my life to be about enduring pain. I wanted experience life more abundantly. I wanted live in a home with no violence and no fear. I wanted my children to know peace, even if I had to build it from scratch. And so I did slowly, tenderly, one breath, one prayer, one truth at a time.

I didn't do this alone. I discovered that God's presence was always with me, steady, unwavering, and guiding, even when no one else came.

Faith didn't erase the past, but it gave me a place to stand and face it. Scripture became my lifeline. Prayer became my refuge. And that quiet, steadfast presence of God allowed me to reclaim my strength, my voice, and my life.

Healing is sacred and personal, but it is also a journey shared in spirit with those who came before me, and with those who continue alongside me.

To my children, you are my heart's greatest work. Every step I took to heal was for you, as much as it was for me. I wanted to show you that love doesn't have to hurt, that home can be a sanctuary, and that your voice always matters.

Healing has required practices. Not just once, but over and over again: breathing through fear, moving through paralysis, connecting despite isolation, and asking for help when in need have become the foundation of my life. They are no longer lifelines; they are rhythms. They carry me, remind me of who I am, and anchor me in love and self-respect.

If you are reading these words and carrying your own story of survival, consider this your invitation: not just to endure, but to truly live. To feel fully. To heal deeply. What was meant to break you can become what builds you. What was stolen from you can be reclaimed breath by breath, truth by truth, moment by moment. Your story is not your shame; it is your strength. Healing is not only possible; it is yours to claim.

When I began this book, I was learning to sit with my

shadows. Now, as I close these pages, I feel the light that has always lived within me. The woman who once wrote from her wounds now writes from her wisdom. I no longer carry the weight of what broke me; I carry the strength of what rebuilt me.

Healing didn't make me forget; it helped me remember who I've always been.

So, as you set this book down, I hope you remember too: your story is not your pain; it is your power. You are not defined by what you've endured, but by how you rise from it. May your own healing remind you that the strongest person has always lived within you.

APPENDIX

Understanding ACEs (Adverse Childhood Experiences)

As I began leaning into my own triggers and writing this book, I discovered the language that helped me understand what had shaped so much of my story: Adverse Childhood Experiences (ACEs). My early ACEs did not simply disappear with time. They stayed with me, lingering in my mind, my nervous system, my muscles, my connective tissues, and even in my heart. They were waiting for me, nudging me to process, to release, and to heal.

Understanding ACEs gave me the language for what I had carried all my life. It helped me see that the pain of my childhood shaped how I showed up as an adult: how I trusted, how I loved, and how I cared (or did not care) for myself.

Because ACEs played such a significant role in my journey, I have included a brief overview and reflection tool. My prayer is that it will offer you insight, language, and hope for your own healing.

The ACE Questionnaire is based on the original CDC and Kaiser Permanente Adverse Childhood Experiences

Study (Felitti et al., 1998). This study revealed something groundbreaking: childhood experiences of abuse, neglect, and household dysfunction leave lasting imprints. They are not "just the past." They affect brain development, the nervous system, physical health, relationships, and even how we respond to stress as adults.

But your ACE score is not your destiny. It is a tool to help you recognize where pain may still live and where healing can begin.

THE ACE QUESTIONNAIRE

Below are 10 yes/no questions that make up the ACE survey. Each "yes" counts as one point. Your score will be between 0 and 10.

While you were growing up during your first 18 years of life:

YES __ NO __ 1.) Did a parent or other adult in the household often or very often… Swear at you, insult you, put you down, or humiliate you? Or act in a way that made you afraid that you might be physically hurt?

YES __ NO __ 2.) Did a parent or other adult in the household often or very often… Push, grab, slap, or throw something at you? Or ever hit you so hard that you had marks or were injured?

YES __ NO __ 3.) Did an adult or person at least 5 years older than you ever… Touch or fondle you or have you touch their body in a sexual way? Or attempt or actually have oral or anal intercourse with you?

Yes __ **No** __ 4.) Did you often or very often feel that… No one in your family loved you or thought you were important or special? Or your family didn't look out for each other, feel close to each other, or support each other?

Yes __ **No** __ 5.) Did you often or very often feel that… You didn't have enough to eat, had to wear dirty clothes, and had no one to protect you? Or your parents were too drunk or high to take care of you or take you to the doctor if you needed it?

Yes __ **No** __ 6.) Was a biological parent ever lost to you through divorce, abandonment, or other reason?

Yes __ **No** __ 7.) Was your mother or stepmother: Often or very often pushed, grabbed, slapped, or had something thrown at her? Or sometimes, often, or very often kicked, bitten, hit with a fist, or hit with something hard? Or ever repeatedly hit over at least a few minutes or threatened with a gun or knife?

Yes __ **No** __ 8.) Did you live with anyone who was a problem drinker or alcoholic or who used street drugs?

YES __ NO __ 9.) Was a household member depressed or mentally ill? Or did a household member attempt suicide?

YES __ NO __ 10.) Did a household member go to prison?

Each "YES" = 1 point. Your score will be between 0 and 10.

Your score is not about blame or shame. It is about awareness.

Higher scores are often linked to more challenges in adulthood: chronic health diseases, mental health conditions, substance misuse, criminal activities, risky behaviors, and struggles in relationships.

But here is the hope: healing changes the story. With faith, therapy, and intentional practices, you/we can rewire patterns and build resilience.

Reflection: Your ACE Score / Story

Take a moment to sit with what you've just read. Remember, your score does not define you, it is simply an entry point into awareness. Use this space to gently notice what comes up for you.

Prompts for Reflection:

- What feelings came up as I read through the ACE questions?

- Did I notice any memories, emotions, or body responses?

- How have my early experiences shaped the way I show up for myself today?

- Where do I most long for healing, safety, or release?

If your ACE score is high (4 or higher), please know this: you are not broken. You are not your score. What it means is that your story matters and your healing matters even more. While ACEs can shape us, they do not define us. Healing is always possible.

If reflecting on these questions brought up painful emotions, please don't carry them alone. Reach out to a trusted counselor, pastor, or support resource. You deserve help, healing, and hope.

REFERENCES

American Psychological Association. (n.d.). Trigger. In APA dictionary of psychology. Retrieved from https://dictionary.apa.org/trigger

Carnes, P. (1997). The betrayal bond: Breaking free of exploitive relationships. Health Communications.

LeDoux, J. (1996). The emotional brain: The mysterious underpinnings of emotional life. Simon & Schuster.

Levine, P. A. (1997). Waking the tiger: Healing trauma. North Atlantic Books.

Martins, D., Tavares, R., & Soares, J. M. (2022). Oxytocin and the neurobiology of attachment: Implications for trauma and resilience. Frontiers in Behavioral Neuroscience, 16(879123). https://doi.org/10.3389/fnbeh.2022.879123

Olff, M., Frijling, J. L., Kubzansky, L. D., Bradley, B., Ellenbogen, M. A., Cardoso, C., … & van Zuiden, M. (2013). The role of oxytocin in social bonding, stress regulation and mental health: An update on the moderating effects of context and interindividual differences. Psychoneuroendocrinology, 38(9), 1883–1894. https://doi.org/10.1016/j.psyneuen.2013.06.019

Porges, S. W. (2011). The polyvagal theory: Neurophysiological foundations of emotions, attachment, communication, and self-regulation. W. W. Norton & Company.

van der Kolk, B. A. (2014). The body keeps the score: Brain, mind, and body in the healing of trauma. Viking.

ACKNOWLEDGEMENTS

My Guardian Angel and godmother, Rena! Where would I be without you? Whew… I had to step away to write this. You have been walking with me since I was 15. When I was homeless at 18 with an infant, you opened your home. You didn't just give me a place to stay, you gave me wisdom, safety, and a vision. You helped me get my first apartment and never let go of my hand. Thank you.

Ms. Lisa, thank you for 86 months, 2 weeks, and 3 days of trauma-informed counseling for victims of crime, sexual assault, and violence. Whew, I graduated from The Ohio State University while in counseling and earned my master's in social work. A degree, I once said, "I could never do what you do." And now, a decade later, I'm doing it. Thank you for every nod and every time you said, "I'm with ya!" and "You got this!" I now nod and tell myself, "I'm with ya, you got this!"

My Two Buds, it has been over thirty years and counting. You stick closer than a best friend! Thank you for sharing your family with me. For our countless noon-day prayers, shared meals, laughs, and the steady prayers still today. You've held space for me in ways only life-long Buds can.

ACKNOWLEDGEMENTS

My Godie, your consistent, constant, unconditional love for me and my children is truly appreciated! Thank you for sticking with me, praying for me, and always encouraging me! May you know your labor of love is not vain and is not unnoticed!

My beyond **AMAZING** friends, you know who you are. I won't list names because you are all equally divine. Some I've known for thirty, twenty, ten, over five, more than two years, or recently this year. No matter the time, you are each a Guardian Angel in human form, and I am Better because of Your Friendship! Your affirmations, love, and friendship helped bring this book to life. I still feel you with me even when weeks or months pass between calls.

Thank you to those who purchased and shared my book. I hope to inspire a survivor of childhood abuse, sexual abuse, rape, sex trafficking, and/or domestic violence to speak their truth, heal, and end the cycle of generational abuse. It is through the release of what has held me in pain, shame, and self-blame that I hope to invite someone to lean fully into those feelings to heal deeply. As you read through my story, may you see yourself as a survivor, not a victim. May you realize you did not and do not deserve to live in fear, pain, or shame. And may you know you can heal and be all that you were created to be.

Don't give up on you or what is possible!

ABOUT THE AUTHOR

Amanda D. Ligon, LMSW, is a licensed social worker, Trauma Support Partner, Decluttering Life Coach, minister, and the visionary founder of No Violence No Victim Inc, a nonprofit advocating for survivors of domestic violence, and Manna's Mission Serving The Homeless Community, her outreach ministry which provides permanent housing referrals and compassionate support for individuals experiencing homelessness, with a special focus on older people.

Born from a raped pregnancy and into homelessness, Amanda is a survivor of childhood sexual abuse, sex trafficking, rape, poverty, and over two decades of intimate partner violence within a marriage. Yet, her story is not one of victimhood; it is one of divine survival, soul reclamation, and purpose.

Faith has been the foundation of Amanda's healing journey. In her darkest moments, when no one came to rescue her, she learned to anchor herself in the truth that God saw her, knew her name, and was walking with her through every valley. Scripture became her lifeline. Prayer became her refuge. And the belief that she was never alone gave her the strength to rescue herself and break generational cycles of abuse.

ABOUT THE AUTHOR

Amanda's work is deeply rooted in both clinical expertise and spiritual truth. As a licensed social worker and advocate, she brings evidence-based, trauma-informed care to survivors of domestic violence and sexual abuse. As a minister, she brings the healing power of faith, Scripture, and the assurance that God is present in every step of the healing journey. She believes that faith and professional support work together, not against each other, and that true healing addresses the whole person: mind, body, spirit, and relationships.

She is a proud mother of four (two sons and two daughters), a bonus daughter, and a beloved grandmother, sister, and aunt. Amanda has been mentoring youth in public schools for over a decade, using her voice and testimony to inspire courage and healing. She has worked with older people for over 25 years in hospitals, residential homes, nursing facilities, and on the streets, always meeting people where they are, with dignity.

Since 2002, she has devoted herself to housing families below the poverty line. As a licensed social worker and advocate, Amanda walks closely with survivors of domestic violence and sexual abuse, offering trauma-informed care and holistic support.

Amanda also creates handmade wellness tools, including herbal bath soaks, facial steams, and natural hair oils, through her healing practice Manna's Nature.

Her debut book, *Triggered to Heal: An Invitation to Feel Fully and Heal Deeply*, is a powerful blend of personal testimony, embodied wisdom, and spiritual truth.

Her companion workbook, *Triggered to Heal Workbook: 16 Sacred Practices to Heal Deeply*, offers the specific breathwork, prayer, meditation, movement, therapy, and grounding practices that carried her from survival to wholeness, all rooted in Scripture and clinical expertise.

Through her words and her work, Amanda offers a sacred invitation to break cycles, reclaim your voice, and remember that healing is possible, you are never alone, and you are always guided by a God who sees you and loves you.

www.ingramcontent.com/pod-product-compliance
Lightning Source LLC
Chambersburg PA
CBHW062224150726

47991CB00006B/2419